THE NINE LINES

INSPIRED BY MY TRIP TO COSTA RICA

TASHAUNA M. RICHARDSON

ISBN: 9781097103676

FORWARD

Ten thousand, twenty thousand, forty thousand, eighty thousand…only three months had transpired as I watched a Facebook Group called "I am Beautiful the Movement" explode with voices of healing words and testimonies. Hundreds of women were sharing the scars of tragedies and the triumph of victories. I was intrigued by the stories, but I wanted to know The Story. Who was the woman who could build such a sacred temple of divine sisterly love? Was she whole? Was she healed? Was she an author or a speaker? Perhaps she was a highly educated Facebook influencer. I searched the group for evidence of who she was and who she was trying to be. Somehow our visions were intertwined. I needed this woman to see what I saw in her. Beauty!

Tashauna Richardson --The First Lady! I found her. I found the architect of the Temple of Divine Sisterhood. She was building in her brokenness. I saw the pain of poverty through the light of what others saw as success. I saw greatness where others saw a history of unfortunate decisions; where others saw a dead end. I held the secret to her beginning. If only she would look into my mirror and see what I saw. Somehow, someway, I had to lead her to a different place; a new space. I had to show her how to be the architect of her destiny.

I found her. I showed her a different way. Together, we began a journey to her financial freedom. Together, we discovered her beautiful. Today she can proudly add the "I am" to her "beautiful."

Tashauna Richardson had discovered her "I am prosperous"; her "I am confident," "I am worthy," "I am independent," "I am loved," "I am free," and "I am

Creative"! She is full and victoriously Tashauna Richardson. Nine areas of growth were born out of nine regions of brokenness.

Welcome to "The Nine Lines" that carried her to places that she never imagined she could go!

Renee Toppin

I never liked flowers until this morning. I woke up with flowers on my mind, specifically, a lotus.

A lotus is a flower that grows in muddy water and rises above the surface to bloom with remarkable beauty. At night the flower closes and sinks underwater; at dawn it RISES to open again. Even in the worst of conditions, it thrives. Sooner or later, the lotus reaches light and becomes the most beautiful flower ever. No one knows the story behind your beauty. They don't know how long you've been waiting for the sun to shine......

I am a Lotus!

--Tashauna Richardson

CHAPTER 1: IN THE BEGINNING

9-27-78 --By way of Dandy Richardson and Colavito Tyson I arrived! I was born in Rocky Mount, North Carolina, in Nash General Hospital. Rocky Mount is a little town split by the railroad tracks. You were identified by which side you lived on. You were either from Nash county or Edgecombe county; there was no in-between.

Hello, world! Tashauna is here; the first of three, the oldest grandchild on both sides of my family. Growing up, I was a little girl of many words. I tended to be feisty, sassy, bossy, and very argumentative. With me, it was never a simple yes and amen. I always had to ask why? I wasn't so much disrespectful; but curious. Well, sometimes, it was rude. Regardless, I had to know why things happened; why they were the way they were.

As long as I can remember, my mother worked in daycare centers. Children adored her. My dad was always working at Rocky Mount Cord Company or his part-time job, "Ye Olde Fish Market." Because of this, we never had time to do "family stuff." I didn't even know what family stuff was! What we did have time for was the church! If it didn't involve the church, it wasn't a priority.

During the summer, I would go to my grandmother's house and read the Britannica encyclopedia to find places I could say I visited. The places in that book were too extravagant. No one would ever believe I went to Thailand. My only other option was to copy other people's summer vacation stories and tell them as my own. I would listen to story after story. If it sounded fun, I would think, "Yes! That's the one I'm taking". Yep, I too went to King's Dominion! I couldn't get up in front of my classmates and admit that I hadn't done anything. I would walk back to my seat, wondering if my teacher believed me. I didn't care. The lie, itself, was satisfying. Then, one day, it wasn't a lie anymore.

My parents took us to Six Flags Over Georgia. We finally were doing family stuff! The trip from North Carolina to Georgia was about seven hours. It seemed like it took us forever to get there!

My sisters and I played your typical road trip games. However, "Mailbox" was our favorite. Mailbox was a two-person game, so my younger sister couldn't play. She was in the middle. The object of the game was to yell out mailbox; claiming the house that it belonged to as your own. The bigger or, the prettier the house, the louder we would yell. Unfortunately, our game was short-lived. I guess we were being too loud and getting on my daddy's nerves!

Looking back, I realize this could've very well been a teaching moment. Nevertheless, neither one of my parents turned around to confirm that yes, we too could have a home like the ones for which we wished. They didn't tell us that we could go to college, get a great job, and possibly earn a great living. We were told to BE QUIET!

Eventually, we arrived in Georgia. The anticipation of what was coming filled our minds and hearts with joy! Finally, we pulled up to the hotel. We were told to stay in the car; at that time, I guess you couldn't have more people in the room than those who were checking in. We sat quietly as we were told, looking around, and ready. With excitement in our eyes, we couldn't wait to get to the amusement park the next day.

The long road trip left all of us very hungry. McDonald's was on our mind; however, my mom had a cooler packed with bologna, a loaf of bread from Piggly Wiggly and those vacation bible school hug juices chilling on ice. Those were the best bologna sandwiches ever! Did we complain? No, we did NOT! We didn't know the sacrifices made to get us there, and we were not about to ruin it!

Morning couldn't get there fast enough. We woke up like it was Christmas. We were all eager to get to a place we'd never been! Oh Man! We rode every ride we could ride and some rides twice! That was a great day! It was also the first and last family vacation we would ever take.

I had friends who didn't have two parents at home. Kids use to say things like "you got both your momma and your daddy in the house"; like it was something special or weird. What they didn't seem to understand was that we struggled just like everyone else.

As a child, I knew we were struggling because I remember the "what did you do with the money" arguments. They were mixed in with the "why are you always at church" ones. I don't remember ever missing a meal or having the lights turned off, but I do remember my friends who lived in single-parent households wearing the best clothes and shoes and I couldn't understand how they did that.

We dressed "nice." We wore dresses every day. I remember wanting the Guess jeans, the Reebok Classics, The Duck Head shorts, and everything else I would see the popular kids wearing. One holiday I opened up a J.C. Penney catalog and daydreamed page after page. I circled that jean skirt and those K-Swiss sneakers. Oh, how I smiled as I wanted every piece of clothing. I never wanted toys; just clothes.

I spent many days at the park playing with my sisters. Being the oldest of three had its perks, but it was also a headache sometimes. I became accustomed to setting an example for EVERYTHING! Still, we shared a lot of great times. From the sharing of clothes leading to fights to me becoming the hairstylist trying to do their hair, we grew up together. Every one dubbed us as Collie girls. Here come the Richardson sisters! We dressed in lace and patent leather shoes accessorized with pretty bows in our hair on a daily. That was our "look"!

Growing up in church, we didn't have much choice. No pants, no nail polish, dresses had to be below our knees, and our heads had to be covered at all times whenever we entered "the House of the Lord"! Winters were the worst! We would be standing outside looking "extra saved" with a denim skirt, tights, and socks over the tights; the whole armor!

One morning, I remember, I was so ashamed of my outfit! I hated my dress because It was the ugliest. Covered with horrible designs and drenched in a sad blue color, it made me cry my eyeballs out. My ma was unbothered by my shenanigans. I just knew she was going to allow me to change clothes. Sometimes I hated her yard sale finds. Can you believe I'm addicted to yard sailing now? Go figure! Let's get right to the shoes. They were patent leather, platform and they reminded me of Pee-Wee Herman's shoes from Pee Wee's Playhouse! I grabbed my book bag and proceeded outside to wait for the bus. I stood there, contemplating how I was going to miss school!

I decided to motion the bus driver to keep going; he did! Excitedly, I ran in the house to tell my mom that I missed the bus. Anything to get out of wearing this hideous dress. To my surprise, she replied," you gettin up outta here!" So much for my plan, because as soon as my dad got home from work, I was on my way to school!

After a while, my dad couldn't take it anymore. We complained about being cold in the wintertime. We couldn't participate in field day activities because we couldn't wear shorts. I was one of the fastest runners in my class, and so was my sister. Do you know how devastating it is to watch other kids have fun? One day my dad said enough was enough! He told us to come with him. He took my sisters and me to get some long pants, as he called them. We headed to

Golden East Crossing Mall. My mom didn't go, and we didn't know where to begin! My jeans were all wrong. I had a pair of fit and flare jeans that made me look like I was straight out of the seventies! I tell you we were clueless when we were out shopping, but mission accomplished!

After a long day of shopping, we always finished by stopping by American Cookie Co. for our favorite peanut butter cookies. Finally, we had traded our holy attire for some long pants. Pants were and still are considered to be men's clothing by some. My dad didn't care because his girls were happy. We were NOT going to freeze another winter. Not on his watch!

Going to school was fun. I was chosen to work with the school's newspaper staff, giving me a chance to interview teachers and administrators about upcoming events and students for excelling in various ways. Having a press badge and a hat made me feel important. The confidence it gave me was just the boost I needed, but I still felt nervous.

I had some great teachers. I can name more than ten, but one teacher was the first person who made me believe in myself. She was firm but loving. She allowed me to go the extra mile. She was the teacher I didn't want to disappoint. With caramel skin and beautiful dark, black hair, I thought she was terrific! Who was she? She was Vanecia Rushing, my 2nd-grade teacher at Braswell Elementary School.

Every morning, I was attentive and eager to learn! She made me feel smart. I loved being a helper! Boy oh boy was it a big deal to be called on to erase the board! That was equivalent to winning an Oscar! I couldn't wait for report cards to go home. I was so anxious to read the "teacher comments"! It would read that I was a joy to teach. That made me feel like a million bucks. My mother would sign her name. I stood there, time after time, hoping that she would respond in a way that would let me know she was proud. Soon, I had gotten so used to the signature I could easily duplicate it.

I was never the student that needed to study a lot. All I had to do was listen. I was just like a sponge, and once I heard the teacher go over a lesson, I was good. But there were days where I wasn't listening, not by choice. My mind would drift off to other things, such as an argument before school. I wasn't my best on those days, which caused my grades to slip often. As I got older, there were times that "the signature" would come in handy! It was convenient at least until I received a zero. A zero required a signature and a phone call! Damn, almost got away! Getting away was only a temporary fix. I was willing to take the whooping and punishment. I wanted to make my mom proud. At this point, anything to not cause a fuss. So to avoid the consequences until I caught, I forged her name. It never dawned on me that I was getting used to escaping and not focusing on the problem! Something was missing. We had the necessities; however, acts of love did not exist in my home!

I started paying attention to other mother/daughter relationships. I didn't have that, but I wanted it! I wondered to myself, "How do you get that? Why doesn't she say it? Why doesn't she greet me with a hug when I come home from school?" I mean, there were times when I wanted to be one of her daycare children! They had it made in the shade! Dining at The Carlton House as a

4-year-old had to be life! I remember they all went to One Hour Photo at the mall and took pictures. I was like, "wow!" She never took us to do things like that!

We spent summers at Buck Leonard Park. Time was spent hanging out at the swings and in the dugout at the baseball field religiously running back and forth to house for water. Only for my mom to say either you're gonna stay in or out! The night began to fall, and there's nothing like a summer breeze after 90-degree weather. Our legs would be "ate up" from mosquitos. We had no care in the world.

These were the good old days! I remember that as soon as the church across the street posted its vacation Bible school sign, we already knew my mother was going to make us attend. I also remember each of us having a dollar to go swimming at Sunset pool. There were also days we couldn't go because we didn't have that dollar. I sure did enjoy Ms. Pearl and Mr. Randy out there under that shed at the park. Man, best of times! From a game of Checkers to Candy Land was the most fun. But nothing compared to catching fireflies and storing them in a jar. Nothing. The highlight of our summer. My mother would yell out our names one by one. We would ignore the first and second call, but never a third. The third came with consequences. The aroma of fried chicken would fill the air. All the kids were hoping it was their mom. Only to find out it was ours. Best fried chicken ever.

In the Richardson household, Sundays belonged to God. As faithful members of the church that looked like Sportsworld, we no choice but to attend. I loved it. We woke up to the sounds of Rev. F.C. Barnes or foot-stomping and coordinated moves of any quartet group. My dad loved them all, but there was something about The Mighty Clouds of Joy that would get him fired up. Before we knew it, he'd grabbed the broom acting as if it was a microphone and was hitting every high note to Walk Around Heaven. The sizzle of red hot sausage frying definitely would make you put some pep in your step. Smother it between two slices of Merita light bread with a thin line of mustard was indeed Heaven.

You couldn't go wrong with a foam cup filled with Bright and Early orange juice. My mother dressed us one by one, and

The "Vaseline" ministry was in full effect. Dressed in lace and bows, we were off to Sunday school. Another service followed at 11 am. and one more at 7:30 pm. I don't think churches do the Sunday night services anymore, but this was our Sunday. I kept my purse full of composition paper to play hangman and tic tac toe because it was an all-day event. I managed to play on the low and not make a move while the preacher was preaching.

Our ushers were top-flight security. One look and they escorted you to your mom. There was nothing more embarrassing than getting caught and having to take that walk of shame! You knew that because of your behavior, there would be no asking to go home with anyone, and whooping was waiting for you when you got home. If you were in the youth choir, it was a plus. Oh, how we could sing. I was a strong alto. I spent those Sunday's screaming from the top of my lungs with no control. The more they hollered sing babies, the louder we screamed! These are moments I will never forget.

Middle school was about to begin, and couldn't wait to change classes and have

my own locker. I
sure why I did it
instruments in t'
trumpet. I signe
asking my pare
the band as an
not me too?"

All banc
instrument on the first day of school. My
parents knew that. The summer before I
started my first year at Parker Middle
School had passed, and I still had no
trumpet. There I was, returning to school,
with no instrument!

I went home and passed the message
that if I didn't have my instrument in a
certain amount of time, I would have to
choose another elective. The majority of the
class already had theirs. I had my workbook,
but no instrument.

"Why is this happening?" I thought.
"It's just a trumpet! Daddy, please go get it!"
After a few days of pleading, I got my
trumpet! I knew they couldn't afford it. Our
house was small, and we overheard a lot of
things. Arguments about money were ones
that we heard often.

My mom and dad were fussing about her getting her hair done, and if you know anything about a Jheri curl, well, they were not cheap. All I heard was I know you didn't pour soda on me. My mom was so angry, and I began to get mad too. An entire 3 Liter Top Pop soda was his choice. I had just had enough. They had taken their argument from inside the house to outside by a tree. I jumped up, picked up my trumpet case, took my trumpet out, and kicking open the screen door, stomped out of the house! With anger in my heart, I got as close to my daddy as I could. Swinging that case as far back as I could, while biting my lip, I wailed on his back with no resistance and no remorse. I wanted him to hurt and to know it was me hurting him. I hit him over and over again. Then, I stood there defiant and waiting, my stance saying, "I dare you to do something to me. I wasn't scared; not even a little bit. He didn't hit me; he didn't say one word.

At that moment, I felt like a champion. I couldn't enjoy that feeling, however, because I couldn't help thinking, here I am, a sixth-grader, and if I could do that to my father, why couldn't my mother?

In my mind, I was like…" why is it so hard for her to fight back?" In my head, I was screaming, "here I am, less than 100 pounds, and I'm defending you! I'm tougher than you are! Kick his ass!"

Music became my escape, and until this day I'd rather listen to music than watch television! My parents took care of me, but I didn't feel love. That void would eventually turn into seeking attention from boys! I just needed validation that at least boys saw me. I wasn't sexually active, but I wanted the kisses, the hugs, the holding of the hands while walking down the halls.

I was looking for someone to occupy my mind to take my mind off home. It didn't matter whether they whistled when I walked by or took notice of my big chest, which led to the nickname "Hooters," I loved it and hated it! I was waiting to hear, "you're pretty," without "you're pretty to be dark-skinned." That was not what I wanted, but it was good enough!

I guess things got a lil' better. We moved to 615 Rose St. It was a bigger home, a much nicer neighborhood and I got to stay in the same school. "Wow!" I thought.

"Maybe things were not so bad, after all."
Lil' did I know; a big blow was brewing!
Things were going on in our home that I
wasn't a part of. There were whispers behind
closed doors and conversations about
actions that no one shared with me. I was
on the outside of whatever was going on
inside, and I hated it. Family is a word that
should have meant we shared it all; the good
and the bad.

I knew some bad things were
happening, but nobody included me. I felt
alone. I was a child, thinking, "somebody
tell me something!" But, there were no
direct answers. My next thought was, "Let
the rebellion begin." Time out! Flag on the
play! Game Over! Years would pass before
I understood what happened.

My parents divorced. I didn't care. I
adjusted very well, considering he didn't
move far...literally. I'd never seen my
parents love on each other, kiss or show any
affection (other than their wedding day)
anyway.

My dad was gone, and life went on.
Seem like we were already dysfunctional as

a family anyway. I wanted to be mad, but I couldn't.

My mom started leaving us home alone a lot! Choir Rehearsal was the destination. We were old enough to be on our own at home, but it still bothered me. I felt isolated. I also felt responsible for my sisters. We had groceries, so I learned to cook. Some days it would be fried Bologna sandwiches, and some days it would be burnt fried chicken. You all know that kind of burnt chicken that was black on the outside and red in the middle. I would tell my sisters to eat the "done" parts! They did. It didn't matter what it looked like or how it tasted. I was gonna cook, and they were gonna eat!

Hours of being left home alone actually forced me to grow up. I began to have unapproved company at home. I calculated my mother's return down to a science! Each time, her absence was more extended than the last. Eventually, she began to stay out overnight.

I was angry as hell, but I couldn't find the words to express my feelings. Well, I could have found the words, but, as a child, they would have been disrespectful! One night I tried to mimic a scene from The Cosby Show. It was the scene when Bill & Claire moved the sofa in front of the door after Vanessa didn't come home by curfew. It was my sisters and me at first. Then, they both said they were scared. As for me, I had no fear at all. I stayed. Tonight was my night. I had made up in my mind that my mother was going to hear from me. I couldn't just stop at blocking the door, and telling her how I felt about all this hanging out all times in the night. I had to take it further! I had the nerve to grab the tape recorder as if I was gonna "trap "her.

Let me tell you! When my mother walked through the door, you would've thought she was Hercules! This 5'4, less than 150-pound woman moved, the oversized sofa (with me in it), with one hand. She pushed the couch out of her way, and back into its original position with no sweat! She ruined my entire plan, and the joke was on me! On that day, I realized that she was grown and I had better not ever do any crap like that again. I had tried it! It may have backfired, but I definitely had tried it!

What was going on outside of our home, eventually moved in! He was someone I had looked up to, and highly respected! Married with a family, he was now living with my mother, my sisters and me! I hated it! The very sight of him made me cringe. Because of their indiscretions, my life completely changed. Things as simple as the kind of bread we ate, going from white bread to wheat because that's what he liked, changed quickly. It wasn't right, and I knew it. But, he was here, and now I wanted out! At school, everyone was picking on me. Our church was 'the" church. All the kids knew what was going on, and they all were talking about it. "So he and yo momma go together?" "Is that yo new daddy?" was all I heard as they laughed at me.

Conversations that were had at home by grown folks in our community were being had at school by their children. I was still a child, but all of this hurt me. It became so overwhelming that I began to join in with the kids who were laughing at my mother. Nothing they said was untrue. I just had to face it. I had to distance myself from what she was doing. The way I chose to deal with it was to go from protecting my mother to protecting myself. I was so angry with her. I decided that if he was gonna be in the home, I was not!

My love for school was dying. I went from making straight "A" s to merely being present. My attitude changed, as well. I developed an "I don't care" state of mind. I felt that if those who should care about me, didn't, why should I care. I wanted to respect the rules, but I no longer felt like I had to. I started asking myself, "Why should I come home after school?" "Why should I do my homework? "If no one was there, who was gonna miss me?" This behavior worked until I blatantly disrespected him.

Every day I grew more and more bitter about this new living arrangement. I remember being very angry. My attitude towards anything and everyone was horrible. I recognized it, but I didn't care.

Because I couldn't follow the rules, I often was on punishment. This time they grounded for at least 30 days. I had to come straight home after school, no phone, no television, and I could only come out of my room to eat or use the bathroom. It was like being in solitary confinement without the bars and barbed wire! He was walking through the hallway, talking to me. I have no idea what he was saying, but I know it aggravated me enough to lock my door. I kept thinking to myself that this is a man that I use to respect, and now he lives in my house, and he is not my daddy. What gave him that, right? I took out my "Gold -N- Hot" flat irons. Those of you who do your own hair know how hot they get. I walked over to my door where he was standing, twisting the knob. He kept trying to talk to me, but I didn't want to hear anything he had to say. My punishment was because of him. How do you go from being the person I thought so much of to the one who was about to catch this heat? I wanted him to leave me the hell alone!

Let me leave this house! As I had this thought, I realized that it could be the best decision or the worst decision! Unfortunately, before I could put a plan in place, my mother decided for me! I came home one day, and all of my belongings were on the front porch. My bed, mattress, dresser with clothes still in them, shoes and all! He had won! My mother's words still ring clear today. "You can't be disrespectful and live under my roof!" There was no need to fuss or cry because she was right; however, I felt unwanted. He was still there. He was the reason why all of this was happening! I called my best friend to come to get me. I grabbed some clothes out the dresser that sat on the porch and went to her house! I don't remember how long it took for me to realize it, but it was clear that I was on my own. Eventually, I roamed from different family member's homes until I wore out my welcome! I needed a job, money, and to provide for myself. Wendy's hired me as a cashier. I enjoyed the working drive-thru and the salad bar the most.

Working at Wendy's on Sunset Ave would be some of the best times of my life! It was my escape from my troubles. We had so much fun calling out orders over the microphone! I met some of the most fabulous folks. I was kind of spoiled too. The days I had my hair done, it was drive-thru for sure. My getaway was work, and I enjoyed the crew. I was even in my manager's wedding.

Eventually, I started hanging out with new friends. However, hanging out with them made me happy. I felt accepted, satisfied, and even loved! They were the "in" crowd. They were popular, dressed well, and when one of them got their license, it was like we all did. I remember one time when we skipped school; we ended up either in Raleigh or Virginia. I knew skipping school was wrong, but it was the era of "if everyone else is doing it… I am too! "Yup...this is it! These are my friends! Let's skip school; let's do whatever! Let's have fun! I sought validation and needed attention! It made me high!

I had a few school crushes, but no one ever took me seriously. At least, not the ones I wanted to take me seriously. I wanted the popular guys. I wanted the ones that everybody else wanted. I could never fess up and make it known on my own. I had to force my friends to tell whoever that I like him. Even that didn't work! I wondered to myself, "why were they overlooking me?" I had long black straight hair, and let's not forget big boobs! These two things usually won boys over! Of course, for the wrong attention.

At a young age, I realized being "in shape" mattered. I didn't have the shape I wanted, but for Heaven's sake, I was smart! I was in accelerated classes! As time moved on, I would find that schoolboys were way too immature to notice everything I had going on. I realized that I had to take it up a notch! Taking it up a notch caused me to start missing days in school. I was never stupid, but I was making stupid decisions. I was sent to live with my dad, and my life was getting worse and worse.

After moving around for a while, I was able to come back home. The man ended up returning to his family, and I was glad! However, it didn't take long before my shenanigans would start.

I was always looking for an escape. I found one. One night while at work, I was introduced to this guy. I could see him whenever I wanted. I didn't have a license or a car, but I had Rocky Mount City Cab on speed dial. He was funny, and I liked his rough around the edges style. He had his place, and I was there a lot. I even started cooking there, doing whatever I wanted. I can't remember how long we "saw" each other because we never claimed a title. He was able to come to my house too. He would leave large amounts of money on my dresser at my request. The opportunity to go out of state was presented. It was a great idea to me. I was seventeen, young, and dumb. I found myself saying "yes" to anything to be with him. I don't even know if he was feeling me like I felt for him, but I didn't care. A few friends joined us on this journey. He gave me one last chance to stay at home. Nope, I was packed and ready to go (with my mother's luggage)

It was the most tiresome and sickening trip ever. I was sick as a dog! We traveled through weather changes; from snow to rain. It was disastrous. At one point, I wanted to get out and walk home. However, I was trapped in that car for hours. There was no cell phone or Facebook to entertain me. No one could keep up with my whereabouts. Stupid wouldn't you say so?

We made it to our destination, and I dreaded the ride back home. Eight hours from home, we get pulled over by the police. I was asleep, and I woke up to blue lights. One by one, they removed us from the car. We were in the middle of nowhere, handcuffed, and placed in separate patrol vehicles. I was terrified. I had to use the restroom badly. A lady officer escorted me to what looked like a trailer in the middle of a cornfield. I just knew they were going to let us go. The charges started with speeding and then off to jail we went.

They gave everyone a bond except me. All I kept thinking was I'm never getting out of here. I'm seventeen, and I've ruined my entire life. The last person I wanted to call was my mom. She told me not to go, but I went anyway. I called my aunt, and she said I had to call my mother. I didn't know what to tell her. I wasn't ready to face the "I told you so" conversations. I waited, and they processed me into jail. I felt humiliated as they asked me to remove the wire from my bra. They even tried to remove my weave, but my girl bonded the hell out of my hair, and they couldn't. I was glad! Next, they placed me in a holding cell with other female inmates. What a damn circus!

Slapped with a color-coded wrist band, they were coded based on the charges; it didn't look like I was going anywhere. The other inmates in holding kept saying that I had a felony. Some even said I was too pretty to be in jail. Jail has no respect of person. Pretty or not, I was behind bars. We were interrupted from our conversation as pimento cheese sandwiches were thrown at us. I hated that cheese; I don't even like grilled cheese. I'm gonna die of starvation. They were already telling me not to drink the grape Kool-Aid. I tried to remain confident that someone was coming to get me. However, I did this to myself. Sitting there ashamed, I felt hopeless and helpless. I placed so many collect calls that it wasn't even funny. I was embarrassed to say my name for the recording so the receiver would know that it was me. Tears began to roll. Then the famous prayer fell from my lips. God, if you get me out of this, I promise jail won't see me again.

After so many hours of not posting bail, the process of going from a visitor to an inmate begins. The next step is being led to what they called pods (cells: your residence until you post bond). I was in Pod C. They put me in a cell, and I had to dress out. I was handed an outfit with shoes, and no this was not New York Fashion Week material. For the first time in my life, I was wearing an orange jumpsuit. It was beginning to be real. I was an inmate with felony charges. I was the property of Shelby County. For sure

I was getting out, but how would it happen and who was going to help me?

The officer woke me up and said Richardson; you have court in the am. I was used to watching people chain ganged coming into court and felt that had to be the most awkward feeling. I couldn't sleep knowing that that's what I was facing. I'm 17, and all kinds of thoughts are running through my mind.

Morning came, and we lined up against the wall. I followed the instructions. The correctional officers weren't mean, but I didn't want to give them any trouble. I was waiting to be chained up to go to court (as I'd seen on television), but that never happened. One by one, the guards took us into a small room. There was a T.V. hanging from the ceiling. What the hell is going on, I whispered under my breath. It's called T.V. court. T.V. court is when you speak to the judge via television. Everyone in the courtroom can see you, but you can't see them! I listened as he read my charges and I added a "Sir" after every "Yes". I didn't know what each charged meant; the judge gave me a $30,000 bond. $3,000 and I could go home. Now, where in the world was I going to get $3,000? I heard that my mom had been up all through the night trying to get up the money to get me out.

I can't imagine what she was feeling, as a mother, knowing that her daughter was in jail. In 48 hours, she posted my bond. After 8 hours of waiting to be processed out, my fingerprints didn't match. Why? My hands were sweating from all of the anxiousness. Everything was pretty overwhelming. I was free again. Thank God! However, I would have to deal with court dates. For the first time, I had to catch a plane. This was no celebration or a vacation. I was going back and forth to plead for my life. The charges were substantial, and yes, I made more than one wrong decision. I was terrified of planes, but I had no choice, fortunately, after several flights and impromptu court dates. Thank you, GOD ALL charges were dropped.

Trying to put the past behind me, I started going to church in Wilson, NC. with my mom. I didn't want to go, but I didn't have a choice.

After all the trouble, there was still a void in my life. Grown men started showing interest in me, and it didn't take much to grab my attention! One whistle, one look, one hello, and the grins began! I fell head over the hills for this one particular guy. He was fine, tall, athletic, and grown! I felt like even if I didn't have all of his attention, I had some of it and I didn't give a damn. He liked me, and I liked him.

It started with us paging each other (we didn't have cell phones then), and his friends were some of my family! We went from friendly conversations to overnight stays at local hotels. Even if it was for a moment, it was my moment.

I had no idea what his feelings were for me. I never discussed a relationship with him. As far as I knew, he wanted what he wanted, and I was willing to give that to him. I did whatever I had to do to stay out of the house!

This free lifestyle led to more men. However, I grew to love and adore this man. He was much older, and I was underage when we met. However, when I turned 18, it was the beginning of a full-blown relationship, at least in my mind anyway. He was a laid back kind of guy. I wanted rough; I wanted the street. He was a good guy, but eventually, I drifted off, continuing to look for what I thought I desired. I justified this behavior by reminding myself that he was too old for me anyway.

Still working my part-time job, I was asked to participate in a joyous occasion. I'd never been a bridesmaid, so I was very excited. I saw someone new, and he'd seen me. He was tall, dark, and married! He never mentioned his marriage to me until it was too late. He reminded me of Gerald Levert. He was well dressed and very persistent! Did I say charming? He, along with a few others, was after me. It was the year of 1998, and I was only 20 years old. I never wanted him or any of the others because I was dealing with someone. He, however, was determined to place himself in my presence at all times. I went to the bathroom to change clothes, and as I walked out there, he was, again. What the heck?

I'm not a good dancer at all, but we danced the night away two-stepping to every song. He kept reminding me how beautiful I was. He said that I was the prettiest "black" girl he'd ever seen. As he grabbed me closer, he whispered in my ear that I was going to be his. He was so confident, and I assumed maybe he'd had too many drinks.

Eventually, he persuaded me to begin a somewhat long-distance relationship. This guy was hilarious, but he was also obsessed with me. One night my best friend and I went to dinner at Applebee's, and I knew he was on his way into town. However, I was hanging out with my best friend. I told him where I was and had no idea he was going to pull up. The way he showed up made me understand his level of obsession. He wanted me to leave her and come with him immediately. I told him I would call him later, but from my window seat, as I looked up from eating my riblet basket, he was standing there with his face smeared against the window. He was standing there, staring at me and it was RAINING!

I continued to eat, unbothered until I realized that he wasn't going anywhere. He just stood there. Why? He kept motioning me to come on. He wasn't leaving without me, and I knew it. I laughed! My friend couldn't believe it, and I couldn't fight it anymore. I walked outside, he opened the door for me, and I left with him.

He started to travel to N.C. a lot. He even sent for me to come to him. I went. More than thirty days passed, and I had to break the news to him. I told him to come to me, and he did. He picked me up from my mom's house, and I swear it felt like I couldn't breathe. My heart was pounding. I think he knew what I was going to tell him, but didn't want to say. We rode around until I was able to say it. Why is the first question always, "well, what are you going to do?" Dammit, what the hell are we going to do! I didn't know!

This man had a whole family, and honestly, our relationship was not going well. Here I was, pregnant by a married man. Several thoughts came to mind. Thank God I didn't give in to any of them!

At 20, I was pregnant with my first child. I promised myself time and time again that I didn't and was not having children! I was angry, and I was happy. Regardless, there was no turning back. Of course, he would say that wasn't his. That's what they all say. Hell, I was a little confused myself. I was dealing with someone else too.

I decided it was best to look for another job Lady Footlocker hired me. While working there, I met Melissa. Working at the Bellsouth kiosk in the early 2000s, Golden East Crossing Mall was the place to be, and she was amazing to me. She could see everything from that lil' booth. Melissa was just a few years older than me; we would find ourselves laughing together on lunch breaks. I even remember hiding from some guy in that lil kiosk. It was great fun. We started hanging out. She loved to travel, and I admired her classiness. We became the best of friends. She watched me go through hell! But, unknown to me, this would be the beginning of my "going through."

As I continued to work at Lady Foot Locker, I decided to move out with a roommate. I thought this was an excellent opportunity to be on my own with my son.

At the age of 21, I had my first child. My water broke as I was eating a Hardee's sausage biscuit in bed. Terrified, I rushed to the hospital! As soon as I arrived, it was "go time!" On March 28, 1999, after hours of labor, we had a son. The man that I was dating declared that he wanted a DNA test, and I complied. The test confirmed, by the margin of 99.9999%, he was the father — his identical twin! This little person would forever change my world. Javan Emanuel arrived, and I was clueless. Motherhood wasn't in my plans at the time, but there was no turning back. I decided to move back home with my mom as I saw no signs of no support I had to result to child support. After nine months and thirty days after I believe that's enough time to wait and "see" what someone is going to do. I had to do what I had to do.

I was fascinated with dressing my son up with outfits from The Children's Place and boy did he have the sneakers to match! At an early age, I noticed Javan's big personality and love for church! It seemed as if one visit led to him desiring more! He loved going so much that he had the church directory. He could call others to take him when I didn't feel like going. Nothing or no one stopped him from attending. He was nicknamed Lil' Bishop and was always front and center with his godmother and other mothers of the church. He knew every song and put down a piece of shouting.

In Pre-k he wanted to dress up as a Pastor for the Halloween Parade. He didn't want to wear a tie. He wanted that white bishop's collar. So, I made one that fit through his button-up shirt. It worked, and he approved! With his New Testament, green covered, hotel Bible, he was on his way. That boy loved God with every fiber in his body.

One night we were watching a movie, and they played My Girl by The Temptations. He burst out singing along. His voice was very soulful with an old-time gospel tone. During every family gathering, everyone would ask him to sing a song. Singing made him happy so happy! On Sunday mornings, we started with BET Gospel. Javan could learn a song after listening to it a few times. It was magical watching this lil four-year-old belt out songs by Mahalia Jackson and a favorite from The Temptations "My Girl." How I Got Over by Mahalia Jackson became his signature song. He sang it in the morning, at school, at the bus stop, and to whoever would listen. He participated in a talent show at school and received a standing ovation. From there he competed in every talent show and won!

My son made a name for himself. Lil Bishop. Church's started calling me inviting him to sing. Not only was he a great singer, but he also began speaking. We practiced sunup to sundown until his speeches were to perfection and memorized.

Life was treating me fair. An opportunity presented itself to me to have a place of my own and "take over the rent." Of course, I said yes! It was perfect timing! Everything was coming together. Aqua Court was almost perfect. There was a daycare across the street, and I finally felt like I could breathe. There, in 2001, I would welcome my second child; my first daughter, the most beautiful little girl ever!

I was working at Reeds Jewelers and doing ok. She had this gorgeous mole on her cheek and charcoal black, curly hair, and I fell in love with her immediately. Jewel Emani was the name I gave her. A very soft-spoken child, she was observant at all times and became her mommy's little shadow. Her laugh was contagious! I said to myself, "that's it — no more children!"

My days were spent taking care of them. Everything seemed to be going well. I had a son and daughter and a pretty decent job. I still had no car. I was trying to make it! Unfortunately, month after month my rent was being paid later and later! One day I left to pick my mom up from work, and as I returned, I had to move out the way for fire trucks. I had no idea they were on their way to my apartment. I had left a candle burning.

Displaced, I ended up moving in with my mom again. I didn't want to do it and hated it. However, I had nowhere else to go! As an adult who had experienced living on her own, having to go back home was a blow! I couldn't wait for them to fix my apartment so I could return home! Bills were still coming, and I couldn't keep up. I was stressed the hell out! My daughter wasn't even two months old. People navigated me to Red Cross, and they helped out a lot. I felt like a case. I felt needy.

On top of that if you know anything about the utilities in my hometown then you know they are incredibly high! The utility bill became so high that I was there several times with no electricity. It was so cold, and it was nothing I could do except wrap them up extra good. Javan was under at least five comforters. All I kept asking him was he warm until he fell asleep.

I felt like a failure. I couldn't even keep my children warm or keep the lights on. Everybody said they would have helped after the fact. Yeah right! Pride didn't keep me from asking for help. It was the conversations had about me asking for help that I didn't want to go through! You know the, "Ain't she working" questions and the, "Where are the dads" questions. The sad part is that as soon as you get through the storm, those who talked trash would show up with "Why didn't you tell me? Girl, you know I would've helped you had I known." I call those people, pop up friends. They are the ones that show up when they think they're missing out or after the storm is over. Never during, always after. At the end of every day, I had to allow God to navigate me through those dark and weary nights for I knew trouble didn't last always. Sadly, it wouldn't be the last time I would face hardships, I would, but I made it through that time. And then the doorbell rings. Who's there? Another problem!

CHAPTER 2: WHAT ARE THE ODDS?

Once again, I needed a place to stay. I could no longer pay my rent so back to the country. I went. The house we moved into was full already, but it was my only option. We slept where we could; the floor, a chair, it didn't matter, we were in and not out. This house was a family property, and I knew not to make this my permanent residence. I was told in advance to find somewhere else to go because the house needed to be emptied, but I didn't have anywhere to go. Everyone was moving out, and the house was becoming more and more empty. I was asked several times what I was going to do, and I didn't have an answer. I'll tell you, living in family property was the worst. Months passed, and I was still there. I fought through the winter with baseboard heaters and boiling water on top of the stove. I have no idea why the boiling water, I had seen my mother do it.

There was nothing in the house but my grandfather's bed. I paid the light bill and did what I could. I felt horrible. I felt helpless but never hopeless. I had a friend that I met in cosmetology school take me to apply for Section 8 housing. I knew I couldn't afford rent, so I needed something based on my income, which was nothing at the time. I filled out an application for Rolling Meadows Apartments. Because of the size of the apartment I needed, they told me that it could be months or even years before something would become available.

A family member harassed me about my exit from the property regularly. I bought time by reassuring her that I would be gone soon. The pressure of being evicted by a family member was worse than that of a stranger. I didn't have it. After a few weeks of "waiting." I called section 8, and still, there was nothing available. I knew I had to do something different; something that could change my life for the better.

Growing up, I'd always desired to be a hairstylist. I kept my curling irons on just in case I had the opportunity to use them. I kept up with the latest styles, and finally, I encouraged myself in the middle of my

struggle to go for it. I was going to
cosmetology school! By the time I decided
to go, there was only one more day of
registration left. With no one to take me up
the street, if I wanted this, "Pat and Joe"
were going to have to get me there. It was at
least 85 degrees outside. I don't wear shorts,
so I grabbed a t-shirt and a pair of jeans, and
slipped on my flip flops. With my papers in
my hand, I started on the three or four-mile
walk to the college. It was hot as hell. A
few tears dropped from my eyes as I was
walking. One car after another flew past me
leaving clouds of dust as only a country road
with red dirt could. I kept walking, hoping,
and praying someone would recognize me.
As soon as I lifted my head and wiped the
sweat from my face, a man stopped and
asked me if I needed a ride!

I jumped in as fast as I could. The ride
took about twenty-five minutes off my
walking time. Difficulties arose soon after I
arrived at college. I didn't have a high school
diploma, but thanks to attending Edgecombe
Community College, I was able to obtain an
adult high school diploma. They even
approved me for financial aid. I figured that
this was the time to make something of

myself. I felt as if this was another chance to do better. Finally, I was registered! I was so excited to go purchase white scrubs and sneakers. Most of the time, people asked was I a nurse or in nursing school. It wasn't easy at all. It was just the three of us, my two children and me, and I was determined to take full advantage of this opportunity.

Javan attended Red Oak Elementary school. However, my daughter needed a sitter. I couldn't afford daycare, so every day it was a constant struggle to who was going to keep her. My oldest son can account for days when I didn't have a sitter, and they would have to sit in the waiting area until I finished. Nope, they weren't supposed to be there, but I had no one to help. I kept going.

Eventually, I was able to find a sitter, and things were starting to become routine. Meanwhile, I kept calling the rental manager every day and probably twice a day when the news hit my heart that we had to go! Let me tell you; I called him pretty much desperate and begging. Explaining my situation, he said well you were bumped up due to the applicant before you finding a residence. Praise break! The next question was, "when can I move? I'm ready right now!"

Finally, after being approved, we moved into Rolling Meadows Apartments. It was right on time. Financial aid checks were released, and I went to purchase a car. I didn't have a license, but I bought a car; a Beretta! I never got stopped, but the battery went dead, and I couldn't even afford to buy a battery. It sat until I sold it. I made stupid decisions; I just carried on.

Move-in day came, and the girls from my cosmetology class helped me move my few belongings. My kids had their own rooms, and they were delighted. I didn't share where I had moved because I didn't feel the need to do so.

The first night was very peaceful. I pulled the mattress into the living room and pumped up the air conditioning! I think I was smiling in my sleep. I looked at my two children and tears started to flow because they were all I had and I was all they had.

I was slowly becoming accustomed to the HUD housing lifestyle. The inspections and the drug dealing in the neighborhood became my new normal. I've always found joy in cooking for my family, and I couldn't wait to burn in the kitchen! I couldn't wait for the food stamps to kick in every month so I could fly to Walmart! Boy oh boy, it was on and poppin' when I learned that Sam's Club accepted EBT. Summer days were spent, sending my children to the park while I fried chicken. It was never just fried chicken. Of course, we had rice and gravy, macaroni and cheese, and my favorite LeSeurs sweet peas! Don't forget the grape Kool-Aid! It's crazy, but I found myself acting like my mom, raising the kitchen window, screaming at the top of my lungs that it was time for them to come in and eat. I'd call their names one by one just like my mom used to call my sisters and me. You should've seen how fast they would take off running. I guess that's what my fried chicken or baked spaghetti would do for them.

     Craving for love and attention, I dipped back into an on and off-again relationship. Wasting no time, I was pregnant with my third child. Neither one of us planned this. I just wanted to complete my hours and graduate cosmetology school on time. I knew that having this baby was going to be difficult for me. Early into my pregnancy, we were off again. We both moved on. I was pregnant during the winter months. It was cold, and I would walk to the bus stop to catch the RMT transit when I needed to go to my doctors' appointments. I felt sorry for myself, and I had not a single soul to blame. The baby weight was weighing me down. I was sluggish and grumpy. As my due date grew closer, it was becoming more and more unbearable to stand in class and accept patrons, but I couldn't stop. I had come too close to the finish to throw in the towel. I kept going right up to my daughter's birth. After a day of grocery shopping and ending my day with Chinese food, I decided to take a bath. A few minutes later, I went into labor.

My aunt was there and called the ambulance to come to get me. Of course, any action in my complex caused folks to go outside to be nosey. I was ready, but I was in so much pain. The EMT personnel asked every question you can imagine. Single, married or divorced? Single. Do you have any children prior to the one you're having now? Yes. How many? Two. Do you smoke or drink alcohol? No, neither. Thank you, Jesus, we arrived at the hospital. I was immediately hooked up to the monitors. My vitals were great, so I was ready to get the party started! I was alone in the room when I delivered my third child. In a few hours, the three of us became four. My beautiful baby girl Jordan Faith arrived February 25, 2006. She was a doll baby with the prettiest little lips and piercing eyes that watched my every move.

I was still unmarried and had no boyfriend. Thankfully, Jordan's dad was there for us when we arrived home. Everyone wanted to see her and hold her. All of that was short-lived. I had no time to bond as a mother. I couldn't afford to take six weeks off. I just couldn't. I stayed out long enough for one doctor's visit, and I begged my instructor to let me return. I committed to going during the day and night to get the hours lost while on my brief maternity leave. She complied. I worked hard even when I was in pain. I couldn't complain because this was the life I created. I dealt with it.

I was getting closer and closer to my 1500 credit hours to graduate on time. Thankfully, I graduated in May 2006 from Nash Community College. I'm not gonna tell you all a lie, after graduation I wanted the flowers, the balloons or maybe a graduation dinner. None of that happened! However, my family was there, and I was grateful for that. I quickly registered to take my practical test. It seemed as every question asked on that exam was something we never went over. I was extremely nervous, but I passed.

With my temporary license, I was able to start my career as a cosmetologist. I was so eager to learn; however, I was afraid of not being the best stylist. I didn't know how to do styles that other stylists were doing. I didn't even know at the time what I was good at, but this was what I wanted to do since I was a child. I met some long life friends while in the industry. It was tiring, but I had no plan b.

Not even a year later, I reunited with an old love, and here I go again. Nothing ever was new. A blast from the past and wham bam thank you, ma'am July 30, 2007 baby number four arrived. At this point in my life, I began to think that I was dumb as hell or trying to make a career out of having children.

After giving the first three children names starting with "J," I couldn't think of anything for him. I called him Sean Elin. Now it was two and two. I said no more children, and I believed that would be the case. Two boys and two girls were enough! This parenting thing was much more than I had bargained for!

That was a big lie! As usual, there was an introduction to a new man; he was never a love interest. Nine months later, on November 7, 2009, Journey Nevaeh was born. I have no idea what I was thinking! I asked myself, "what the hell are you doing, Tashauna?" Again, I had to quickly adjust and keep it moving as I'd always done. I knew I wasn't going to receive help for her, so I kept working. I even found a second job during the holidays to attempt to make ends meet. I don't think my ends have ever met each other. It was a hard struggle, but I refused to complain. After about a year child support kicked in. I received thirty dollars a month. Sometimes it was only thirteen dollars. These were my children, and I was solely responsible. Begging had never been my thing, and I was not about to start.

I had no one to blame for my situation; it was all my fault! I replaced hurt and love with babies! I cried a lot of nights trying to understand why was I repeating this cycle that was weighing my body down. Mentally, I was drained. As the old folks say, this was the bed I'd made so now I had to lie in it. I began to believe that to be true. This was my life, and I couldn't do anything to change it. Once you become complacent, it's hard to even see outside the box.

However, there was still something on the inside that made me feel that greater was in my destiny. What was it? Who's going to take me seriously? I had five children by

five different baby daddies. I was still a
recipient of government assistance. I
allowed myself to become accustomed to the
crumbs, and sadly, I dealt with it. Life
wasn't slowing down for me, but I continued
to press on anyway.

CHAPTER 3: HUSH LIL' BABY DON'T YOU CRY.

While working full-time as a hairstylist in Oakwood Shopping Center located in Rocky Mount, N.C., I would take numerous breaks next door to Maxway. The store was therapeutic for me. If I ever came up missing, people knew to look there first. I probably stayed there more than the salon. It was nothing for me to walk out and always see familiar faces because everyone knew each other. Oakwood was the place to be! All the business owners in the strip got along. We became so comfortable we would even bring folding chairs outside to watch the cars go by and catch a breeze in between clients.

I started to notice that at almost the same time each day, this guy would be pulling up or leaving. I'm thinking to myself, what man needs to come to Maxway every day? One day I was outside, and he rode by giving me this stare down of a look. I said this guy is crazy, but he's also rather cute too. As I was standing outside, I saw him again. He was passing out flyers for an event at a local club, in the strip mall where I worked. We saw each other, and he made sure he gave me a flyer. I said, "no, thank you, I don't go to clubs." and he said, me either, but I want you to come to this tonight. I took the flyer and said, ok. I told him I needed a ticket for my friend too. Before I turned away, he asked, are you coming? You would've thought Kem or Lyfe Jennings (two of my favorite artists) were coming; the way we flew to the mall to shop for a new outfit!

I was excited! Anytime I decided to go out, which was not often, I planned on having a great time! My friend picked me up, and within seconds of our arrival, I spotted him, and he spotted me too. I took a seat at the table and began to look around. The band was jumping, there was a nice crowd, and he made his way to our table. He politely asked if I wanted something to drink. "Water, please," I said. My friend took my picture and he decided to photobomb it. With a smile, he said I hope you didn't mind. It was over from there! He had a beautiful smile. I couldn't believe I'd never seen him around considering I've been in Rocky Mount all my life. Well, it didn't take much after that smile for me to want to know more about this guy with these beautiful locs. We became Facebook friends, and things quickly escalated from there. Our conversations about life were deep and intimate. My days of assuming were over, so I asked him was he single. Of course, the answer was yes. After several conversations, we decided to go out a few times. Eventually, our relationship became sexual.

After the newness wore off, and I realized he didn't want to pursue anything serious with me, things started to fade. A few months went by, and a lonely night led me to call him over. I didn't even want sex, but that was the hook! I desired companionship. In minutes he was knocking on my door dressed in his nightclothes, including bedroom shoes. The kids were fast asleep, and I led him to my bedroom, hoping he would hold me, but I knew what he wanted. Honestly, I just "laid there." Afterward, he said damn girl you just laid there like a corpse at Hunter Odom Funeral Home. I couldn't help but laugh.

He turned his back and went to sleep. I grabbed a shower and jumped back in the bed. Maybe I should have participated that night because a month later, there was no sign of a period! Guess what? I was pregnant. Here I go, a-fuckin-gain is what I said! At this point, I've made this into a career. With no one else to blame, I was making it an even six!

I wanted a relationship. I knew, however, my child's father did not. I kept trying and pressing the issue. The void that I spent my entire life trying to fill was still empty. Even after all of the men and all of the children, nothing in my life rid me of that feeling of emptiness. Silent depression kicked in. I didn't want to go through another pregnancy alone. It was that moment that I'd realize I'd been good enough to have sex with, but no one saw me as worthy of anything serious. So, I began to question if this was how people viewed me? The answer was always; it's not you; it's me. Cue the violin! Do you know how many times I'd heard that shit! The question I had to ask myself I was how did I view myself.

Of course, the answer was "desperate." The most I had been to any of them was a "baby mama." I'd never been engaged nor married, and I quickly accepted the fact that I may never be. I began to be ok with that.

Time was flying. When I stop pressuring the issue of a relationship, things began to come together. I was calling quite often to have baby conversations. I realized that that was the most I could ever expect from him. So I settled and accepted what he gave me.

He wanted a boy, and I wanted another girl. I would stop by to let him see how big I was getting. I wanted him to be involved. I was always trying to be considerate of others, and I thought that if I named the baby after him, maybe he would become excited. I thought about the tattoo on his neck, which read Khalid and immediately came up with Khaliyah. He loved it! I was trying hard to win him over, so I began referring to the baby by name, Khaliyah.

By now, I thought I was a professional at "telling" what the gender was, based upon the shape of my stomach. I was very anxious to get to my ultrasound appointment at Nash Day to prove me right! I sat there patiently waiting for the nurse to call me back. I saw a nurse come to the waiting area. She glanced at her clipboard one more time and said Tashauna Richardson. I jumped up and followed her to the room. I laid on the table, shirt up, and as soon as she placed the controller (or whatever you call it) on my stomach, she could immediately tell what I was having. She told me to look so I lifted my head and stared at the monitor. The cursor circled his identifying parts. With joy, I said oh my goodness I can't wait to tell his dad! It's a boy! This baby was his first son!

He was happy and nervous when I gave him the news. I expected a more significant reaction from him, mainly because I knew he wanted a boy. The farther along I got into the pregnancy, the more attention I desired from him. He'd give in now and then to keep the peace. I wanted what I wanted, but I compromised and allowed him to handle me on his terms. We remained cordial as best as we could. I kept him in the loop with every appointment. He even attended the baby shower, but I could feel the disconnection. I felt as if he didn't want to be there, and as soon as it was over, he was gone. He didn't even ask if I needed help cleaning up. He was gone. I didn't care; I was happy he showed up.

My due date crept up on me. Then, it passed me. I was overdue! My due date was adjusted, and on Jan.19, 2012, I woke up knowing that was going to be the day my son would enter the world. My children quietly slept as I got dressed. My sitter came up, and we rehearsed the children's morning routine. I whispered to her that I'd be home soon; in and out!

At 4:45 am, I arrived in the parking lot. At 5 am, I checked myself into Nash General Hospital to be induced. I kept telling myself I was never doing this again, but then I was reminded of the last five times I had uttered the same words. This time, however, I had already made arrangements to have my tubes tied.

Five minutes later, I was dressed in my luxurious hospital gown with peepholes in the front and back, and again, the process started with me being there alone. Lying comfortably in bed, I wanted to rest or perhaps take a nap, but I still had to be "mommy" to my other children. I grabbed my phone to make sure they didn't oversleep and got off to school ok. A few hours passed and was hooked up ready to rock and roll. I was known to pop 'em out in a few hours so I just knew this one wouldn't be any different. I dozed off and woke up to The Price is Right and a knock at the door. It was my mom and stepdad. I had gotten so used to delivering alone it felt strange to have visitors. It wasn't a big deal anymore.

I was anxious. Eventually, the nurses added Pitocin to my I.V. to speed up my contractions. I have a high tolerance for pain, so I was like bring it on! The doctor on call came in to see how far I had dilated and determined I was moving right along. In between breathing and checking my phone, my son's father walked in. Immediately, my world was alright. I smiled on the inside. His presence mattered. His first son was about to arrive, and he was front and center. I had one request. He stood at the foot of the hospital bed with three tubes of Victoria Secrets lip gloss. That's what I wanted, and that's what I got! I was impressed.

Hours passed, but there was no baby. No worries! I was a professional at this! He was being stubborn. I got this! The pain started to become unbearable. I reached my breaking point. I requested an epidural. The epidural was supposed to ease the pain, but it felt like the pressure was winning. I was still dilating, and I kept reminding myself that I'd done this before. "Get it together, Tashauna," I said to myself! I was miserable. I looked over, and his dad is chilling and relaxing. His new wheat Timberlands were placed nice and neat against the wall. His were feet resting on the ottoman as if he was on vacation. Oh no, this ain't that type of party. If I can't rest, you can't either! Put your shoes back on NOW! Did he put them back on? Of course not! Till this very day, we laugh about this moment.

The doctor came in bearing the same news. "You're nine centimeters; almost there." I was nine centimeters four hours ago! More than thirteen hours had passed, and I was exhausted. I was feeling defeated. My cousin, a nurse, came in to comfort me as much as she could. I went from the rocking chair to bouncing on a ball to pleading for pain medicine.

Eventually, the doctor became a tad bit confused jokingly asking, "Where's your baby? Did he travel up to New York?" He calls for an x-ray machine, and what we found out made me mad and relieved at the same time. My baby had a short cord, so he was bungee jumping, having a good old time.

At least 20 hours had passed, and his dad stepped away for a few. As soon as he left, they wanted to speed things up! They said we needed to do an emergency C section. This entire process could have been over if they would've just checked. I told them to wait for his dad. Hell, a few minutes wasn't going to hurt I'd been in labor since the day before. They didn't wait, even though I wanted him there to see his son being born. They immediately prepped me for surgery! I was scared because this was the first delivery by C section. I didn't know what to expect.

Frantically laying on the table, I looked over at the clock and noticed that it was after 3 pm. They told me to take a few deep breaths, and I could feel myself going out. Even though I was fully medicated, I could still feel the pressure of the delivery. I caught myself moaning in agonizing pain. I told the doctors that I felt the pressure, and they said you couldn't have, but I did! Today I have absolutely no feeling where I was cut.

I slowly awakened, and I looked to my left. I saw my son; my sixth child. January 20, 2012, my son had arrived. He was perfect! The hours of hard labor were over! I looked at his eyes. He was quiet and calm. They whisked him off to the nursery, and I couldn't WAIT to ask them what in the world that was all that about!

I was ready for that mommy baby talk; I needed to smell him. My mom and sister were waiting too. They had a chance to see him more than I did. Everyone was saying how much he looked like his dad. I couldn't agree more. I even heard the doctor say so I see where he gets his forehead from. We all laughed. My body was numb, but I was anxious to see him. We waited patiently to hold our son. His dad and I laughed a lot about my labor shenanigans as we waited.

After about an hour of waiting, there was a knock at the door. It was a knock that I will forever remember. I sat up as the door opened. I made sure I was comfortable enough to hold my son. At the door was his pediatrician, but my baby was not with her. I looked around, but there was, no nurse and no baby. My heart dropped! In that very moment, I was shaken. She said the nurses attempted to give him a bottle and it would come back up immediately. She was 100 percent sure she knew what that meant. I didn't. I thought he needed another kind of formula. The diagnosis was Te Fistula! He couldn't swallow! From that point, everything was a blur! He had to be airlifted to another hospital. Another hospital? Suddenly, I was scared and crying uncontrollably. It was happening all too fast to grasp.

My child's father and I had to be strong for one another. We didn't understand; our child looked perfectly fine. Identical to his dad. I was able to obtain enough strength from somewhere to be wheeled to the nursery to at least look at him. He showed no sign of pain. I gazed into his eyes as long as I could. I started feeling weak and helpless. Tears flowed from my eyes like a river though I made no sound. My entire body felt dismembered. By the time I made it back to my room, the aircrew had arrived. They wheeled him into the room so I could see him one more time before he took his first flight; a flight he would take without me. I grabbed his blanket to put over him. They kept reminding me that it was warm in the incubator, but as a mother, I could only think about it being cold outside. I had to make sure he was warm enough. He looked fine; almost perfect! I wanted to leave with him.

I asked my nurse if they could transfer me to the hospital with him, and she told me no. I was on a hall full of mothers bonding with their babies. They were being showered with "It's a Boy" or "It's a Girl" balloons and gifts, and here I was empty-handed. I could hear the cries of babies, and I wanted mine. He wasn't there, and I wanted out! It was torture. He needed me, and I needed to be there!

Jan. 21, 2012 his dad went to be with him, and I was anxious to hear how he was doing. He couldn't send pictures fast enough. All I could see was a perfectly healthy baby, but he wasn't! I had to make a lot of decisions over the phone. I knew nothing about Tracheoesophageal Fistula. I googled it right away and watched every video I could. The nurses asked questions, and I trusted that every yes I gave was the right answer. I was desperate to leave. Whatever they wanted me to do, I did.

As I prepared my mind to get to my son, my doctor came in with more bad news. What the hell is it now? Ms. Richardson, you lost too much blood during your C section, and we have to immediately prep you for a blood transfusion. Do you mean with someone else's blood? Yes, she answered. I was falling further behind mentally, physically, and emotionally. I quit. I can't do this anymore.

The nurses brought in several bags of blood, and the transfusion began. They wrapped my legs to prevent blood clots. Hopelessness started to kick in. I grabbed my phone and looked at my picture of Ja'Kari all the while thinking whose blood is this? All kinds of thoughts raced through my mind. I whispered at the picture on my phone and quietly said mommy's coming. I was so involved with his health that we hadn't named our son. We had that "J" thing going, after a few minutes of deliberating, we decided to call him Ja'Kari Khalil McBride.

Three days later, I'm released, and I can't wait to get to Greenville, NC to see him. Unable to drive, I depended on my son's father to get me to and from the hospital. I could barely walk, so they utilized a wheelchair to transport me through the hospital. His dad was patient with me. From needing assistance to the restroom to taking me grocery shopping the very night of my release, he did what he could to make this situation easier for me.

The very next day would be the beginning of a new life. I was anxious about seeing my son again. For me, the visit was very confusing because I didn't understand what was wrong. They escorted us to the Neonatal Intensive Care Unit, and he couldn't wheel me fast enough. As we entered, I could see his little head. I wanted to hold him right away. With care and being guided with his monitoring cords, I was able to do that. I brought blankets from his baby bag to wrap him with, and to leave in his dresser. I stared at his face. Again, he looked so perfect. The doctor, we were told, would be over soon to answer all of our questions. She walked in, and her smile was so angelic. She had diagrams and explained everything with clarity!

Can this be corrected, I asked? Yes, she said. We're going to take good care of your baby. My body was growing tired, and my legs swelled every night and after every visit. Days leading up to his surgery was very nerve-wracking!

It was surgery day. I didn't get much sleep the night before, and I was growing weary by the second. Morning came, and we left for a 30 min ride to Greenville, N.C. We decided to go early to be able to spend time with him before surgery. We arrived, and as routine, his dad pulled up and grabbed a wheelchair, parked, and met me back inside.

Anxiously awaiting to hold him, the nurse laid him in my arms. Without a care in the world, he looked so peaceful. It was now time. I was surprised they allowed me to hold him as we were escorted to prepare him for surgery. There, the entire surgical team greeted us. We either hugged or gave a handshake to each one. Lastly, the doctor showed up, and she greeted me with a hug. She prayed for us and said God has us covered. As she reached for my baby to take him back, I lost it. I wailed as my heart broke into millions of pieces. My body shrunk. I kissed him. I held him as tight as I could; considering the tubes. All I could do was sit there. I wanted to run, but I couldn't. How do you be strong when your baby has no idea what's about to happen? I heard the doctor's voice again; God has us covered.

His dad allowed me to cry as much as I needed. I can only imagine what he was feeling. The hospital gave a device that notified us of the progress in the operating room. From the time of anesthesia was administered to his vital signs, we were updated minute by minute. They even sent a few messages about how cute he was. Being wheeled off to the cafeteria to wait was the worst. As the hours passed, my legs were swelling from all of the sitting. I never said a word. The TV was on in the waiting area, but I couldn't hear a sound.

Finally, his surgery was over and successful. Everything seemed as if it was going in slow motion. The nurses briefed us on how heavily sedated he was, but his vitals were great! Every nurse reminded us how handsome he was, and his surgery was a success! We couldn't touch him. We could only look through the small opening in his incubator. All I could do was pray and cry. This little bitty baby endured so much pain and was going through it like a champion. He had on his cool shades and the cutest decorative bandages. I started to reflect on my condition and realized I could be going through worse. Here's a baby that's not even 30 days old and has been through more trauma than I've ever been through in my life. His next step was recovery. They started removing different tubes as he began to heal.

We were there every day. My mom packed up and moved in with me for a while to help me recover my C-section and take care of my five other children. I don't know what I would've done had it not been for her. She does owe me a few groceries, considering how many times my smoke alarm went off due to her cooking. They offered us the opportunity to stay at The Ronald McDonald House, but unfortunately, we were unable to spend one night there due to home obligations. It would've been great to have been directly across the street from the hospital, but I had children at home to take care of as well.

Every day, my son was beginning to show enormous amounts of improvement. We received a call that he had been released from NICU to his own room. The doctors were ready to introduce him to the bottle, and we were front and center. After a few attempts and confusion, my son latched on, and he was a pro! Swallowing, something we take for granted was my son couldn't do. However, now, he was doing it. I cried with joy. We were ready to feed him. His dad and I took turns; both of were excited to be a part of his healing.

On 2/13/12, with special instructions, we were able to walk our son out of the hospital. It was going to take a year for total healing, but he would be fine. The doctors told us that if we saw any signs of discomfort to bring him in every time. A lot of doctors' appointments were ahead of us, but we were ready. We couldn't wait to tell him about all that he conquered.

Usually, two days after having a child, I'd quickly jump back into life — not this time. Learning to co-parent was extremely hard. I needed to go back to work because of business obligations, but I had a son that needed my undivided attention. I sought out at home, sitters by making a Facebook post. Thank God for a great friend who responded saying she was able to watch him for me.

After a few weeks at home, I noticed complications with his breathing, and we rushed him to the hospital. From the visit, we learned that he needed access to at home breathing treatments. I made sure he received his treatments twice a day. Challenged with business responsibilities and maintaining a household of six was extremely hard. I called Word Tabernacle to have my son dedicated, or some may say christened. It was a beautiful ceremony. I asked a photographer to come to capture as many pictures as he could. Immediately after service on my way home the brakes in my van gave out, causing me to hit the stop sign entering oncoming traffic and crossing the street. My children, all buckled up in the backseat, had no idea what was going on. I screamed Jesus and closed my eyes. No hurt, harm, or danger took place. All I wanted to do was go home. At this moment, I realized that even though I had gone through so much hardship and pain, God was still with me. He was still covering my children and me.

As time went on, my child's father became more and more occupied with other things. He was busy when I needed him to watch Ja'Kari. It didn't take much to upset me. I needed to work, and his lack of support was making that difficult. He was unavailable. I needed help, and I was a few phone calls away from going to social services. My clients would come to get their hair done, and I had to ask several of them to hold him as I styled their hair. Someone suggested that I apply for disability. I did so, but they denied my request. Clients would come in and say they had seen my baby's daddy riding around. How disheartening it was for me to have my son around hair products, knowing he shouldn't have been there.

Unfortunately, I had no help. Weekend after weekend, he sat as comfortably as I could make him in his car seat while I worked to make sure my family had what it needed to survive. I was struggling. With no money to repair my van, I sold it for about $500. Desperate for a few dollars to keep my head above water, I did what I needed to do.

I was emotionally and physically exhausted. I received a letter that I needed to come in for a biopsy. I was dying on the inside, and there was no relief, no pause, no timeouts. Afraid, I didn't know what to do. My thoughts were racing as I wondered if I had cancer, and if I would be able to face the outcome if that was my diagnosis. I called the nurse to reschedule. I need to focus on my children.

Ja'Kari grew stronger every day. But there were always times when he would have an episode of a few days in the hospital for respiratory issues. After a few days of treatment, however, we'd be back to our regular schedule.

I became angry watching his dad take vacations when I was running out of the energy to take care of our son. He became preoccupied with more things and people. There was nothing I could do until I used Facebook to express my true feelings. It was wrong, and I knew it was wrong, but I didn't care. I was tired and restless. It wasn't fair. With regret, I took my post down, and we talked. I apologized to clear my conscious, but I wanted him to feel like I felt. Once I realized nothing was going to change; I tried to move on.

July 18, 2012, Ja'Kari was breathing heavier than usual. After minutes of treatment, I decided to call the ambulance. I phoned his dad. He rushed over. The EMTs proceeded to ask questions and decided that he needed to go to the hospital. All I wanted to do was notify Vidant to let them know we were coming. Didn't care too much for Nash General Hospital at all, but he needed a more substantial dose of treatment to calm his breathing down.

They gave us a room immediately. I looked over, and he was playing with his dad. I was making calls to make arrangements for my other children because his visits were never in and out. The nurse came in and whisked him off for a few examinations, including an x-ray. His dad escorted our son while I continued to make calls to let everyone know what was happening. The request was placed to

Vidant to send a helicopter, and I was relieved.

As I walked out of the room to prepare to leave, my son's room was bombarded with what looked like more than 20 nurses and assistants. I asked the nurse that was standing with me why all the commotion. I could see in her eyes that she knew why. As I quickly turned around, I read the lips of another nurse saying get her out here. I began to scream what are y'all doing to him? My body began to lose feeling. I could see the faces of the nurses and doctors that were treating him. I yelled, "what did you do him!" I took off running of the hospital and ended up laying by a pole in the grass. As I got up and began to walk toward the hospital, I could see the sun was setting. Before I could make it in, the doctor walked toward me and whispered in my ear, "I don't think he's going to make it" — those words repeated in my head for hours. I couldn't breathe. I couldn't stand. I couldn't walk. I couldn't talk.

The word quickly started to spread. The hospital entrance was full of familiar faces. I didn't want a hug or to be comforted. I wanted my son.

After hours of sitting there, I was allowed to go back in and see my son. However, I couldn't touch him. I had to wrap my mind around that, so it took another hour or so. I grabbed a piece of strength and the arm of his dad and began the walk. I felt like I was in a psych ward. Everything looked disfigured. My eyes were swollen from crying, and my voice was hoarse from screaming. One nurse opened the door, and three nurses stood in his room, their eyes holding back tears. There he was laying with tubes in his mouth, eyes closed, and a white sheet to his neck. I leaned in as close as I could and repeatedly whispered his name. His dad behind me for comfort, I wanted my son. I desired to pick him up, but I couldn't. I couldn't do anything. Rage entered my heart. I wanted to fight; to demolish anything or anybody. I walked in the hospital with my son, baby bag, and car seat. I would be leaving without him.

I just needed to be held. My son's father took me home. I asked him to stay. After a few hours, we both realized we couldn't stay there, and he said get up and let's go. I cried as I stumbled to grab clothes. We made it to his home, and I just cried myself to sleep on the couch. I woke up to my best friend Alexseil there. I don't remember her getting there or how she even knew I was there. She said, friend, you were crying in your sleep. She said she turned my phone off because of its constant ringing. I sat up, and I heard the sound of a lawnmower. My son's father was outside, cutting the grass. I didn't ask one question.

I had to recalculate what had just taken place. I walked out of the hospital as a grieving mother preparing to make arrangements for her child's home going. I didn't have insurance, so the community came together on my behalf. Jars were set out, and plate sales were being done in his honor.

There was another storm brewing. In just 24hrs, all hell broke loose, and Ja'Kari's dad and I were so divided. I was being dragged through the mud on Facebook because folk had their opinions about my behavior. I just lost my son; I was angry. There's no correct way to act or feel when you're dying on the inside.

My apartment quickly filled with people I knew and people I'd never seen a day in my life. I was tired. I was exhausted from making decisions. I gave my son's father the task of finding his final outfit as I could barely sit through making his arrangements. The funeral home was not where I wanted to be. I didn't want to answer if we needed a family car and if so, how many.

I didn't want to be a part of the final arrangements. Feeling as if I had died with my child, I couldn't bear all that came with putting him to rest! On the day of the viewing, I was approached about a balance. I could've sworn enough money was raised to bury him. No money was placed in my hands. I panicked because I didn't have it. However, the way was made. We gathered in the lobby to pray before going to see him. His dad and I were given privacy to go in first.

Slowly, I walked towards the chapel. I walked in with my head down, and as I looked up, I yelled as loud as I could. They said it was so loud it echoed, more roaring than 18 wheeler's horn. I held it until I heard myself. I slowly walked down the aisle with his dad, and there he was in a white casket. Dressed in all white, he looked like a baby angel; so peaceful, but his lips were a little darker. It was surreal. My son was dead. I called out his name as if he could hear me. I wanted to run out of there. My mind was telling me to do bad things. I looked up on the screen above his casket, and on it was a video of his pictures with Whitney Houston's rendition of Jesus Loves Me playing in the background.

I pulled up a chair and sat at his casket, not quite believing that this was happening. Let's go back. Let's rewind. Maybe if I took him straight to Vidant, he would still be here. Maybe Nash General hospital did something to my baby. I think they suffocated him with the tubes they placed in his throat. Perhaps it's my fault. I was going crazy, and no one noticed. Maybe I should die too.

Bodies of people were surrounding me with condolences. I didn't want them. I wanted my son. I wanted to see him take his first step. I wanted to hear him call me ma. I wanted to see him enter his first day of school. That's what I fucking wanted! Some tried to take me to dinner afterward. Dinner for what? This event wasn't a celebration; it wasn't a party for me. Take me home. I'm tired. I was receiving notification after notification on Facebook of condolences that it became overwhelmingly depressing. I couldn't function.

July 23, 2012, I woke up dreading the day. The night before I couldn't even find the strength to do my hair. I barely had enough energy to dress my children. I took one deep breath and attempted to get ready. I kept looking around my room, and in every corner, there was something that belonged to my son. His baby bag, a bib, or a new outfit, all reminded me that he wasn't with me. I realized it was over.   Although his dad had stopped by to drop off the printed obituaries, we weren't speaking. He handed them to my mother and left. People started to arrive in my parking lot to line up. I came downstairs in a sleeveless black dress, a black hat that I borrowed from my mom's good friend, black heels, and black sunglasses. I couldn't afford any family cars, so my mother drove me.

We arrived at the church. The funeral home directors began to call out the order to walk in. With a loud voice, he called out "Parents of Ja'Kari" right here. I looked, and I was by myself. I looked around, and his dad wasn't next to me. Instead, he was directly behind me with this woman. She was a woman that I didn't know, but a woman he wanted to walk him in. My family wasn't having it. Tears began to run down my face as I continued to look forward. There was so much chaos behind me that I felt like going back home. A friend of mine who happened to work with the funeral home whispered to me to not look back.

The pastor walked out and told me that he and his staff were there, and I wasn't alone. It was time. I was first in line, and the church doors opened. It seemed as if his casket was a mile away. At that moment I couldn't see anyone to the left or right of me. I heard nothing. A sense of calm came over me, and it felt like heaven lifted me off my feet and carried me to my son. There he was laying. I don't remember if I kissed him or touched his hand, but peace met me at his casket. I took my seat and his dad to one next to me. I watched people walk past his coffin, some turning to his dad offering condolences to him as if I wasn't even sitting there. I watched it all. I watched two families divided during a time they needed to be united. The service began, and his body language told me he didn't want to sit next to me.

I felt it all. Not once did he ask me if I was ok. I counted to 100 in my mind to keep myself from knocking the shit out of him. So many emotions were raging. Our conversations about keeping him while I worked replayed in my mind. After one last opportunity to say our goodbyes, the casket closed for the final time. I wanted to go home at that point, but I couldn't.

At one point in the service, my cousin Dale Harper, a nurse who was present when Ja'Kari was born, came to sit with me. I guess she saw me struggling to stay sane. When she sat down, I took comfort in resting in her arms. I kept wiping my tears with the same balled up tissue until she motioned the usher for more. I probably looked like a cotton ball with the tissue pieces all over my face. Pastor Gailliard's message gave me a sense of hope and understanding of death that I had never known. I understood that to live, death was inevitable.

The service was coming to an end, and I was greeted with quick hugs and cards of condolences. The police officers were awaiting us to take our final ride to the ending of my baby's service. I got in the car and the first question I asked my mom if anybody was there? She said Shauna, yes! From the front to the back and up into the balcony, the church was full.

My baby's service was very uplifting and powerful. I knew heaven was his home. I knew that if I wanted to see him again, I needed to live my life in a way that made that possible.

We arrived at his burial site. I saw the tent. I saw the pastors and other officials waiting for us to walk up. We were seated, and his casket arrived. Tears started to fall because I knew in just a few minutes it had to enter the ground. It ended with prayer, and everyone started making their way back to their vehicles. I was still there. The funeral home associate asked me if I was ok to watch his entrance in the ground. I answered, yes. By far, this was the hardest visual to witness. Imagine the size of an extra-large laundry basket entering the ground and your child is in it. I turned away several times, but my feet didn't move. It was over, but I couldn't move. My son was gone. I went back to the church for the repass and I couldn't eat. I was ready to go as things were not going smoothly. There wasn't enough food to feed everyone, along with so many other things. I tried smiling through it, but I couldn't. I was ready to go home. Family members came over to "sit" with me, but I was mentally drained. My Aunt Neat stayed the night, and for that, I was grateful.

The very next day, everyone went back to their regularly scheduled lives, and it was quiet. A week passed, and I was still washing my son's clothes. I kept his green pacifier out and became angry when I thought my children lost it; only to find out it had fallen into the crease of the chair. His baby bag hung on the door packed with diapers, medicine, wipes, and a set of changing clothes. Seven years later it's still packed. Seven years later, I still struggle with the anxiety of being around babies and being invited to baby showers. Seven years later, Rob and I are great friends.

There are days where we talk on the phone for hours, not point fingers, but simply to remember the great times we had with our son. We are still his parents, and we're not perfect; however, I respect him as his dad, and he recognizes me as his son's mother. It's never been easy, but it hasn't always been hard either. One conversation changed our entire life. When I see my son's father, I see my son. Seeing his face is therapeutic for me. For years I didn't have that because of our feelings. Today all I have to do is call. He understands, and we understand each other. I thank God for him. Our son's body rests in Gardens of

Gethsemane, but his soul resides in heaven
and our hearts.

CHAPTER-4: LIVE OR DIE!

2012 was the worst year of my entire life. I lost a child and had to pick up the shattered pieces of what was left of my life. I didn't want to do it. I didn't feel like doing it. I didn't want to do this thing called life, but I knew I had to live.

My prayer life consisted of me begging God to take me. I was very specific. I'm known to be a hard sleeper, so yes, that's the best way, in my sleep.

Externally I appeared ok. Internally I was decomposing; almost rotten to the core. No one noticed, they all returned to their lives. Everything was wrong, so the only other alternative that could "fix it" was death. I wanted my son. I felt robbed. God, you didn't give me a chance to hear him call me mommy. Why? No one cared. Eventually, the visits stopped. I screamed into the atmosphere, "Just let me die already! My other children will be fine! I'm no longer worthy of being anyone's mama!"

This emotional roller coaster lasted three years.

I accepted what had happened and that I would have to deal with it, but how? Every day I rushed through the hours. Life was taking too long. I tried counseling; it made it worse. His dad and I weren't on good terms at that time, so I was unsure of what to do. God, do you see what's going on down here? It felt like someone was beating my heart with a hammer. I wanted to punish myself for his death. Why did I take him to that hospital? There were a lot of what if's. Why was I still adding his clothes to the laundry? Why was his baby bag still packed? He's never coming back. It seemed as if everyone was asking me to go to baby showers. I tried to attend one, and it almost took me completely OUT. I continued to sit there, trying to put on a celebratory face. I called my mom to pick me up. It took me days to get past that. Afterward, I declined all baby showers. I was falling apart.

It is said that time heals all wounds. I beg the differ. Time is a constant reminder of what was supposed to have been. I celebrated my angel's first birthday with a birthday cake. I thought it would help ease the heartache, but it didn't. He wasn't there. The high chair was empty, and I could only imagine what it would've been like to have him sitting in it. Empty thoughts raced through my mind. I beat myself up again, asking myself why I took him to that hospital. God, why? I was raised not to question God's work, but I couldn't help but do so! I wanted peace, but I couldn't find it anywhere. I struggled to take each breath. Everything was to the extreme. Some days I could laugh, and some days I could barely get out of bed.

My routine became getting my children ready for school, going to the salon, and coming home. There was nothing else I wanted more than my baby. He wasn't coming back, and I knew it. I had to do something and quickly or I would forever be lost. I opened up my mouth and asked God for peace.

I surrendered to life.

I wanted to live!

I wanted my son back!

I wanted my heart to heal!

I wanted my smile to be real!

It didn't seem like any of these things were possible. I continued to sink into myself. Then, I realized I was still alive. As long as I had life, there were possibilities. I had to find a way to pull myself out of the darkness into which I had allowed myself to sink.

CHAPTER 5: NOW WHAT?

There were days when I couldn't open my eyes. The swelling due to the long nights of endless crying had become a regular occurrence. There were days where suicide would be my portion. All scenarios came across my mind. Should I stand on the railroad track? Should I overdose on pills? I was depressed and mentally ill, and I wanted the pain to end. I did my best to present myself as having it all together, but as much as I wanted to feel like I looked, I was dying! No one else could see it; at least I didn't think they could.

Time moved on. In the latter part of 2012, I entered into a relationship with someone that I met on Facebook. He was handsome, funny, charming, and he seemed to understand pain. Honestly, that's how we met. We built a foundation of love from pain. He immediately fell in love with my children. Our relationship developed from a date at The Waffle House to seeing him just

about every day at my house. He had
dreams, and so did I. We had countless
conversations about what we would do next.
We'd set a goal, and then we'd crush it!
Then immediately, we'd add another goal to
our list. After a year of dating, I became
more in tune with his wants, needs, and
desires. In doing so, I slowly drifted away
from myself and the things that made me
happy. I found happiness in the fact that he
was pleased. I remember one cold night as
he was leaving my place, standing there
looking him dead in his eyes and with him
staring back, he said, "Imma take care of
you." I believed him.

In the course of us trying to work out
a few things, I received a letter of eviction
from my apartment complex. Eight years of
me complaining about moving away from
that lifestyle would become a reality. My
eviction date was 12/25/13 Christmas Day.
Damn, another blow! I had five children and
no money saved. I had neglected to report
all my income. I had worked even though I
lived in subsidized housing. I knew it was
wrong; however, everything financially was
my responsibility. Someone presented my
landlord with a picture of the salon where I

worked. I didn't fight it or argue. I asked to go in peace. Walking back to my apartment, I cried, trying to understand why things were happening the way that they were. I needed to do something, so I got up one morning and just started riding. I never made it to work that day. One of my clients called, and I remember telling her my situation. She led me to a house on Cedarbrook. How I got it, I don't even know. Approved for the home, and I needed the money to move in. I called one friend who forwarded me to another. It was yes! She loaned me the money to move. As soon as my tax refund was available, I paid her back!

Finally, I could breathe a little. I was grateful to have people that genuinely cared in my corner. We packed and made many trips back and forth between our new house and our old apartment until it was finally empty. This was a big jump from what we had been used to for the last eight years — finally, a two-story, four-bedroom, two full bath home with a beautiful yard. I never rested so well!

2014 was looking good. My children enjoyed our new home, and we had plenty of space. My dad came over to visit for the first time, and you would've thought we'd moved into a mansion. He was extremely proud.

After seven months of living in our new home, I made one of the worst/best decisions of my life. I moved in with my former boyfriend's house, forty minutes away from my hometown. We talked about some serious changes we needed to make to make it work. I knew as a hairstylist starting over; this wouldn't be the best time to move. So I decided to keep working in my hometown of Rocky Mount. After a brief run working temporary jobs, my boyfriend eventually started driving long-distance trucks. He went back to what he knew would make sense and money. After months of commuting, I couldn't do it anymore. The drive was wearing me down. We discussed the income change I would face starting over in the city where we lived.

I felt like it would be better for me, and for once, he would have my back like I had had his countless times. Well, that didn't happen. He began to treat me as if what I was doing wasn't enough, as if I should be earning the same as he was. He began to act as if being a hairstylist wasn't a real job. He quickly forgot who was there for him to pull him through his dark days and financial hardships. I thought we were a couple, but he started treating me like a roommate. I dressed him up one too many times, and his attitude changed. He started "feeling himself"! I thought he would cover me, but he started complaining about everything! When he came home, I cooked for him — washed his clothes, and I was like damn what did I do?

I never should've left my home, but he won me over with "the schools" are better. Besides, this man was not my husband, and I was not his wife. I don't know what the hell was I expecting? After three years of dating, I knew he wanted out.

He came home with help to remove pretty much all of the furniture. He took my clothes out of the dresser and left them on the floor, snatched the blinds down and exited my life with a "you better find somewhere to go because the house is going into foreclosure!" I sat there and watched him load up, and I didn't utter a word. I didn't cry or fuss; I didn't do anything! I just sat there.

That wasn't the end because he couldn't exit quietly. He needed to make a public service announcement on Facebook. It was public humiliation at its finest! Post after post after post detailed how he felt I had done everything wrong! I received plenty of messages from people telling me what they would do. Thank God I didn't listen. Most of them were playing both sides anyway. Not one time did I retaliate or become resentful. Social Services was called after he turned the water and power off. People reported that I was a neglectful mother by having them live in those conditions. It didn't stop there! He had a badass cheerleading squad cheering him on!

Every move he made was used to attempt embarrassment and destroy me. He craved the attention of the people that once liked us a couple. Damaging me and my reputation became his high. It was if he was addicted to hurting me! As they kept laughing, I kept working. Never once did I hit back. I kept quiet. Amid my storm, I continued to work and focus on protecting my children from the residue of the onslaught of the public ridicule. They didn't understand. All of this was all my fault! I should've never given up my life for his. I had learned my lesson, but at what cost!

One day as I was scrolling Facebook, I came across several beautiful pictures. Each photo was just as amazing as the one before it. Intrigued, I looked for the name of the photographer. He was Marc Connor. I reached out to him via messenger and asked him to give me a call. After the call, I decided to do a photo shoot. I didn't have the money to get all glammed up, but I needed this for me. As the day of the shoot approached, I began thinking about what I wanted to accomplish by doing this.

Marc helped me with that. He gave me one word, and that word was "reflect." I took a moment and thought about all the hell I was going through and released it through my eyes, my smile, and my posture. After an hour of taking pictures on downtown Fayetteville St.in Raleigh, N.C. the shoot came to an end. I received the photos, and all I could say was, "oh my God! "Is that me?" All this time, I was looking to others for strength, and I possessed it. I looked at those pictures over and over, and with each

moment, I was regaining my confidence!
For three years, I had walked around in
chaos! At this time, God made me depend
solely on him for everything! As I trusted
him, I began to feel the weight of depression
lift. I began to live and celebrate my new
found freedom! I had honored myself with a
beautiful photoshoot, and in doing that, I
had honored Him.

Following the photoshoot, I wanted others to experience "that moment," so I decided to allow twelve women to be featured in a calendar called, "I am Beautiful!" It was at that moment that I realized I didn't have to mirror anyone else for strength. I looked at God and myself. I quickly wanted to give back to other young ladies that had been through tragedies such as myself. It was a simple idea; a twelve-month calendar that featured and showcased the impeccable strengths, and stories of local women who overcame obstacles and were self-empowered.

Nov.26, 2015, I created a space on Facebook titled "I am Beautiful...#TheMovement. This movement was designed for women who had triumphed over life's trials, faced darkness, and survived their experiences. The birth of "I Am BEAUTIFUL" began with the loss of my six-month-old son! I had lost my way as a mother and as a woman. This MOVEMENT developed into a conduit that connected women globally throughout social media, thus giving life to all of those who shared and reciprocated sisterly love.

This God orchestrated movement snowballed! In 30 days, over 80,000 women joined. Hundreds of testimonies were pouring in daily. I couldn't put my phone down because I was too afraid I would miss something. The stories of triumph were so uplifting and inspirational. Unfortunately, the enemy attempted to show his face. There were countless Facebook posts made about my group. They encouraged Facebook to shut me down and declared that I was a fraud. Some even went to the extent of trying to host a live protest to take me out. I stood quietly. God comforted my heart with, "to come after you is to come after me." I did this, so they are no longer attacking you; they are attacking me." God said, "I got this!" I rested in knowing that all was well. The group continued to grow, and it became out of hand so fast that I started chapters globally, assigning other women to manage them.

As was trying to deal with this awesome group of women, the home I lived in went into foreclosure. There was nothing I could do. There was no saved money. I had nothing!

Feb.18, 2016, I left the key under the mat. It was all over except my van was in the garage. I was a few months behind on my payments, and it needed some mechanical work done as well. It was tax time, and I hoped to catch up when my refund came. I received a screenshot from Facebook that he reported to the lienholder that my vehicle was in the garage. My friend and I went back the very next day to arrange for my van to be picked up, but it was gone! I stood in the garage looking around, thinking, "you have to be kidding me! Who opened the garage door?"

I was furious, but I continued to keep quiet. I never responded on social media in a way that he knew how I was feeling. So now I don't have a roof over our heads or a vehicle. My whole life was smeared on social media. It was as if I was the headlining act of a comedy show. Still, not once did I respond. I was at my lowest; rock, fucking bottom! He was the same man that said he loved me. He was the one that planted a cross and flowers on my son's grave now he was trying to drag me into one of my own!

Facebook became his stage! He needed an audience, and his followers boosted his ego. I witnessed people that I once respected laugh and side with his behavior. How as a human is it ok to laugh about a mother that lost her child? I began to pray for him because this was not the man I knew. He left me because he wanted to. He didn't need a reason. He made up one anyway. He told worse lies he could create. THEY WERE ALL LIES!

Thank God I had a few people around me that prayed and protected me. There is no telling what I could've been capable of had I been alone. I concluded that I was dealing with something bigger than me. This fight required someone stronger than myself. My life was not my own anymore. I made a decision quickly to press my way. If life was to be lived, I finally wanted in. The days of death were over! I surrendered to God! I was about to ask a question that I hadn't nor did I want to ask. "God, let me talk to you for a minute. Why am I here? I pleaded with you for three years to bring me home to you because I didn't have the guts to do it myself. Because of my religious beliefs, suicide was out of the question. However, the thought of going across a moving train track came to mind several times." I didn't get an answer, but I began to expect one!

I continued to pay close attention to this secret group on Facebook that poured in hundreds of testimonies by the hour. It grew so fast that I needed help with approving members and post. I had never seen anything like it — testimonies from all over the world. In 30 days there were 80,000 women in their screaming I am Beautiful!

Some tried to abuse the group with their thing and thought I should operate it to their liking. My focus was on this group day in and day out! It consumed my life! I had to add three administrators to help me manage it. It was out of this world! Any and every tragedy a woman could go through was represented in IAB. Renee Toppin was invited to IAB and today doesn't remember who, but she was now a member of my world. Renee stood back and watched. She watched everything. With an overwhelming response, we planned our first event. Handle Me with Care! I rented The Rocky Mount Complex. I knew this was going to be huge! Eighty thousand women in the group screamed I'm coming! There was a roar that my city needed to hear, and I was ready to introduce these women to Rocky Mount; my hometown. The event went live, and now it was time to sell tickets and get vendors! I was beyond EXCITED!

It was difficult selling twenty dollar tickets, so I lowered the price to five dollars. Unbelievably, the five-dollar tickets were even more challenging to sell. We asked for $1 donations, and people hit me with what are you going to do with our ten dimes!

All the while, Renee watching it all unfold! I questioned myself for the sake of people. Was this too much for a first event? Was the stadium necessary? God quickly reminded me of why I did this. It wasn't about the people; this was about obedience! God told me to do all of this. The numbers were the numbers. However, I had a faithful few who believed in the vision! They understood what I believed and never redirected the plan. The day came, and it was a day I will always remember!

Did I cross all my t's and dot all my i's? No, I did NOT, but I DID IT! Some people will only talk the talk, but I actually walked the walk. We had a phenomenal line-up — excellent speakers, singers, dancers, vendors, spoken word, and even a mime praise team. As the day was coming to an end, there was an unpaid balance. We ended up having to take up an offering to finish paying the bill. I walked away with seven dollars in my back pocket, but I was satisfied. I did what I set out to do, but I couldn't help but wonder, where was everyone? Why didn't I fill up the stadium? For heaven sakes, there were eighty thousand women in the group! I stood in the middle of the football field. I started to reminisce about my days as a color guard for Rocky Mount Senior High. Glinka played through my head as I performed some of the moves. I stood there as the crew was still cleaning, and I said God; you told me to do this. Wasn't I obedient? I took a deep breath and walked away.

As I walked away, I heard a voice say, "I didn't tell you that you were going to fill up the stands. I just needed you to have faith to believe that you could." Tears began to fall down my face. This event wasn't for my city, as I thought. It wasn't for the group. The event was my first encounter with faith. Seven days later (which happens to be my ex's birthday.) Renee Toppin returned. She ran a visual play in messenger via Facebook of everything that happened my event. Renee watched me struggle to sell five-dollar tickets, and the disrespect people had for me as the visionary. She watched me wave my food stamp card around used to purchase a Patti Labelle pie (which was delicious and worth it). She said, "I want to help you." Why does she want to help me? Who is she? It didn't matter; she was God sent! She didn't beg me. "If you let me help you, your life will never be the same," she said.

I went to her Facebook page. Some of you would've posted who sent you; we have no mutual friends so blocked! That was not my response. When you walk in expectation, you respond differently. Her page was clean, and it looked like she was "somebody." I responded and asked, "what I gotta do?" It was Friday the 13th; go figure. Some probably would've taken that as a sign to quit before beginning.

May 13, 2016 (which happens to be my ex's birthday) I was at the salon, and it was slow due to rain. You know we don't move in the rain, and we especially don't get our hair done. I logged on Facebook, and I sent her a private message. I said I was ready. I didn't know exactly what I was prepared for, but I can tell you that I was tired. I was tired of being sick and tired. I looked at my account then I looked at it again. As I sat in a car borrowed from a friend, I was all in! I joined Surge 365 right away, leaving only a few dollars left in my bank account. I didn't care. I was more excited about what I was going to gain. I felt great about it. My first week in the company, I earned my first on thousand-dollar bonus. It was a "Fast Start" bonus. What that meant was that I got paid just for earning a bonus! I called Renee and asked her when it would arrive. Monday couldn't get here fast enough. I was nervous as I ran to my mailbox and it was there!

I thought to myself, it was so much fun earning my bonus, and I wondered what the odds were of me doing it again? This bonus was more than I was making that as a hairstylist. I QUIT MY JOB the following Monday and folk went crazy! After packing my belongings, I walked into the owner's office, and I waited for her to write out my last check. She handed me a check for

$132.50. I took a picture of it, and I prayed. God this has been struggle money, please give me the strength to show my children stability with Surge 365.

I left it there in God's ear. The world went crazy. Tashauna was no longer a stylist. "She better go back and ask for her job," they said. Please tell me why do we celebrate bondage (a job) but turn our nose up at freedom (opportunities)? My next phone call was to social services! I was making my rounds as I was excited about my new adventure in travel. It was time for my recertification, and I made one phone to say I do not need your assistance anymore. They even called me back to ask if I was sure! It's a sad day when you have depended on the system so long that they are not sure if you're able to feed your children without the assistance.

I wasn't a millionaire, but I was confident that this was my way out. I had found another way. I waited on the 19th of every month for seventeen years to feed my children. Now the 19th comes as often as I want it too. Finally, I took my hands out of man hands and placed them in God's hands. Excited, I posted on my Facebook page about this newfound freedom and oh the noise that rumbled! "Girl, I would've never quit my job" and (evident that I'm not you). "those things don't work!" Some even told me to be careful! I heard it all. Some went to the extent of making Facebook posts about it, adding police emojis as if what I was part of was illegal. I witnessed it all! There were a few that said I have to see you do it first! I decided I would put on one hell of a show, and they never partnered with me.

Friends and family were blowing the whistle on my business: discouraging others from joining because of their self-doubt and ignorance. I witnessed the hate that was supposed to be for me. I felt none of it. I was protected from it all. For once in my life, I didn't care what anyone said. God said go, and he didn't have to tell me twice! I didn't break a sweat. With no consultation nor validation from man, I was 100% sure that this is what I was supposed to be doing!

There are people that you meet in life and some are for a season, and then there are some that are there for a lifetime. I'd known Cranton Justice for over eight years. Something that started on Facebook led to a real friendship. This guy watched life happened to me. He never sugarcoated how I handled some situations. He gave me the real truth, and it even came to a point he had to let me find out things the hard way. Anytime I needed him he was always there on standby. He was one of the few that encouraged me and celebrated every little milestone. He was very proud of I am Beautiful...#TheMovement, we celebrated with a dinner.

It was a sunny Sunday, he let down the top on his Corvette, and I let my hair blow in the wind. Afterward, Renee Toppin called, and he overheard our conversation. Not once was I trying to recruit him, but he heard something that I was excited about and inquired. Traveling was something he was already doing. It made sense in his life, so I quickly put Renee on the phone with him. I heard him ask Renee, " will this help Tashauna? If so, sign me up!" He didn't how much it cost, nor did he watch a video. He really didn't know what he was signing up for. He honestly just wanted to help me. Now that's a real friend, and it doesn't get any better than that! He will always be my number one, and there can only be one number one.

Everyone should have a Cranton Justice in their lives. Cranton's are rare, but they're out there. He wasn't the first person I spoke to. More than sixty were before him, and the first list I handed Renee was family members. One by one, they rejected our offer. At one point, she called me in between making calls for me to ask if I was sure these people were my family members. I answered yes, I'm sure. Happily, my friend Cranton was the first person to say yes! And that's all it took! That one yes was quickly followed by superstars. I couldn't make this up if I wanted too.

My Success Seven includes:

1. Cranton M. Justice

2. Monique Lockhart

3. Shelia Leggette

4. Lolita Chesson

5. Adrienne Dawkins

6. Diana Bryant

7. Laticia Nicole Beatty

We made a run for it! Not fully understanding; but running!

Before I knew it, Renee Toppin was literally living at the Holiday Inn Express in Rocky Mount. She was showing up because my actions matched my words! She knew that I had run out of options. This was my moment to show my children something different. From our first meeting of seven to packed out rooms; I was on a mission, and there was no turning back! Renee had a way with her audience. She spoke life to those that attended the meetings. It was almost like I was at church, and every word in her presentation was a hard truth. Some could take it; some couldn't. Some used the word scam, and some used the words great opportunity. While others were curious but interested; others would make a move. Then, some were the lookie-lookies. They were just nosey! Whatever the response, she could fire back in a way that would have them joining in the end. It was as if she had an altar call!

She validated the future Tashauna while everyone was still trying to tell her about the Tashauna of yesteryear! She didn't care to listen. She recognized greatness in me while others could only see a single mother with five children, living in the system, with six baby daddies. Days when I didn't understand, were accompanied by prayer. My "Mama Bear" protected her cub at all cost. I had no idea that she needed me as much as I needed her! One day she called me and said I have someone I want to you meet. He was my upline Director. Renee always spoke about him when referencing her method of training. Who was this Tiger Trainer? What did Red Eye Nation mean? I didn't know, but I anxiously awaited the call.

It was a Sunday evening when a Detroit number appeared on my phone. At the other end of the line was Nakia Muhammad. Grabbing a pen and paper, I sat straight up! With a solid tone, he said hello superstar. I've heard all about you. My jaws locked up from grinning so hard. He said I'm here at the hospital with my mom, BUT I wanted to make sure we had this opportunity to talk about your next level. For a second, I was paralyzed. My ears heard what he said, but I couldn't understand why he would use that time for me. As he spoke to me, silent tears rolled down my face. He kept talking about me, my life, my children. Although he had called me, I asked was he sure if this was a good time! He said he was doing what the creator created him to do. I was having conversations with myself as he was still talking about me. Who are these people that want to see me win so badly? I had no resume of success. Why me? He explained to me divine connections and sense of urgency. No time could be wasted for what he and Renee wanted me to accomplish. No one had ever earned the $50,000 Bonus in their first 100 days, and I was their choice.

By phone, we had "Backoffice Bootcamp". Step by step, we pulled my top two people. These are your runners. Let's run a play for them and by default you will hit it! Those Top 2 Leaders were Adrienne and Laticia. With the three of us combined, there was no way I wouldn't do it! Before we hung up, he said you've started a fire in NC, and my job is to help you keep it burning. That meant he was on the way. Renee planned a "Super Saturday" in Raleigh, NC, and we packed the room. I didn't know what to expect, but he walked in cleaner than the board of health. His presentation was top-notch and paired with

Renee's energy; the entire event was mind-blowing! The room was filled with dreamers who were ready to join or take their businesses to the next level. We all had an assignment. We wall had clarity.

As Nakia says, with clarity there's no confusion. We ate a quick lunch, took a few pictures, and got to work right away. He flew in that morning, and just like that; he was headed back to Detroit. We understood that we had to take this journey and bring as many winners with us as possible. Renee Toppin, The Coach, came with a plan for my life. Nakia, The Tiger Trainer, called the play, and I was the quarterback. No one was ready! My first 84 days in Surge 365, I became its first $50,000 Bonus Earner! I called Nakia. He answered with, "Congratulations! I knew you could do it!" Take care of your children, save your money, and remember I'm always here.

CHAPTER 6: INTRODUCING MS.50K

My office of the day was Starbucks, located in Target in Knightdale, NC. The countdown had begun. Something amazing was happening. In less than one hundred days I was on the brink of becoming Surge 365s FIRST $50,000 Bonus Earner!

Was this really happening? On day eighty, I was wearing the same yellow, "I am Beautiful" t-shirt I had been wearing for a while. I neglected every personal need for an opportunity to change my life. All I could think about was the possibility of what my life could look like, how it would forever change my children's lives. I'd already exceeded my personal goal date, and my mentor kept telling me to get it done already! Sweating, nervous, biting nails, skipping breakfast and lunch, and never getting up to use the bathroom, I sat there, adrenaline pumping to get it done. I glanced at the time on my laptop. It was almost time to pick up my children. I needed 100 people in my team builder group to qualify. I was at a screeching 99. I decided to jump back on Facebook and posted the number "1". My best friend Melissa Thomas called me and said I don't know what you're doing or what you need, but I'll take that spot. My heart began to cry as I sat there, and before I knew it, my eyes were full. The tears started to run like a flooded dam. I couldn't control myself, and my body began to shake uncontrollably! My friend was partnering with me. I thanked her over and over, and then I checked my back office. I needed to look, and there it was; the number 100 was lit up. I stood up, and then I sat back down. I was weak in my knees. My brain was about to explode, and I felt the need to scream, but I couldn't do it in there. I stood up one more time, and made a Facebook post saying, "it's done!"

I closed my laptop, wrapped up the cords, and my charger. In my Payless flip flops, I flopped to the car to the beat of my heart pumping. The grin on my face had my jaws locked. I was so excited that I found myself fumbling with the keys! When I was finally in the car, I let out a THANK YOU

JESUS from the top of my LUNGS! I kept telling myself to calm down because I had to go pick up my children from school. The first person I called was Renee. She had told me not to call her back until it was DONE! I yelled I DID IT! IT'S DONE! She replied I knew you could do it! I knew you would do it! She said go pack, and I will see you in Atlanta for The Tashauna Richardson show. I didn't know what that meant, but I said, "ok." I received calls from the founder to the Co-CEO to other directors of the company congratulating me for a job exceptionally well done!

After so many hours spent in Burger King & Starbucks, it paid off! I'd done countless travel parties, endless phone calls with Renee and now it was happening! I remember riding on New Bern Ave. in 2015. Coming to a stoplight, I heard God say, "what you're going through right now is temporary." We have to stop at red lights (red means STOP) because if we don't, we could injure someone else and possibly ourselves. When God is your navigator, he'll move traffic out of the way for you. He'll clear roads that once were blocked on your behalf. Here I was, a single mother of five children, a woman that once knocked on a neighbor's door not to borrow sugar but to borrow electricity because my lights were off, and I had earned a $50,000 bonus in 84 days!

It was August 2016. My mom, Pastor Jesonya and her son traveled to our first convention at the Hyatt Regency in Atlanta. I didn't know what to expect, and all I kept saying was WOW! People were asking for my autograph, it was UNBELIEVABLE! Awards night came, and all of a sudden, the lights went dim. Renee was invited to join Coach and the other founders on stage. I was sitting in the back. When Renee speaks, we all listen. Her voice and words pierced the heart of many as she gave our testimony. In the end, she said I found Tashauna Richardson. Everyone grabbed their seats as if this had never happened before. A video started to play on these larger than life projectors!

Sixty seconds of my life flashed before my eyes. They even captured pictures of my children. As I walked toward the stage, my knees became weaker and weaker. I stepped completely out of both shoes. I fell to my knees. My entire body was like a ragdoll. I looked up, and Coach Tomer, Scott, and Chris were holding me up to stand. As I was presented with the $50,000 check, God said to continue to give Him all the glory and the days of lack are over. They gave me the microphone, and my first words were, "God, I thank you for keeping me here and in my right mind!

I looked out in the crowd. The flashes of camera phones and the blinking of quick snapshots of this moment overtook my body. There was a roar of celebration in the room. Hope and possibility were introduced to the hopeless. I was the example that it could be done and I was standing in front of them. They said many before me had tried it, but no one came close. I had done it in my first 84 days in Surge 365. I was the first! I didn't have any network marketing experience like some assumed. All I needed was Renee to show me how it could be done, and I put the work behind my word.

The next day my phone was blowing up with people I've never heard of before. The congratulations were coming in so fast I couldn't keep up! It quickly dawned on me that it was coming more from strangers than familiar faces. For sure, I was going to be able to save more single mothers now because I did it! I just knew that the people who knew me and my story would jump in. I was wrong.

The hatred grew more and more! Jealousy and envy had a face, and family and friends mainly wore it. "Y'all can't believe everything you see on Facebook posts," continued to interrupt my timeline. Why was this happening? These were the same people that sent me encouraging messages when I was going through. These were the same people who kept reminding me that it was going to get better. I saw folks posting police emoji's warning others to leave these kinda things alone. I was like, "damn is that really what they think I'm involved in?". I quickly learned that the highest level of ignorance is to reject something you don't understand. I kept going.

Adrienne Dawkins invited Renee and me to her Super Saturday in New York, and under my picture on her flyer, she had the name Ms.50K. All I could think was, "wow!". Then just as quickly, I began to think that maybe I shouldn't be called that. She's the reason why the world calls me

Ms.50K today! Thank you, Adrienne, as you can see I love it!

This new life was quickly beginning; however, I was still homeless. I was grateful that we had a roof over our heads, but it wasn't mine. I sought out a few people that I thought could help me but hit a dead end every time. One morning as I was taking the long commute from Winterville, NC to Wake County, I caught a glimpse of my children sleeping. They were exhausted from the 5 a.m. early morning wake-ups needed to get to school by 7:30 am. I couldn't take it anymore. They didn't deserve this! Tears of disappointment started to roll down my face. I whispered to God and said, "I know you didn't bring me this far just to bring me this far. There was no sign that he heard me, but I started filling out application after application. I was pleading with people to give me a chance. Nothing. The sound of crickets was beginning to be familiar. I received rejection after rejection. I kept saying to myself, "I have money!". Unfortunately, my credit score was shot. I told people that I could pay for the remainder of the year, but no one was listening.

A few people suggested that I pay off the debt I had with creditors and come back with receipts, so that's exactly what I did! Still nothing! After about $500 in application fees, I said forget it! I purchased a 2015 Mitsubishi Outlander and moved into the Wyndham by Wingate hotel in Raleigh with Jewel, Jordan, Sean, and Journey. Javan was in his last year of school. I thank God for the wonderful couple who took him in when they didn't have too. To my credit, at least they didn't have to get up so early and could try to get their proper rest. I hadn't realized the damage I was creating with my instability.

The children loved the pool and the free pizza and cookies on Monday nights. Many days I would come back to the hotel, after dropping the kids at school, and cry because I had money to get a place and couldn't understand why all the rejection. Still, I was grateful. We lacked nothing. Jordan's and Sean's dads continued to pick up their children on the weekends. No matter where I was, they were right there. They gave me the same respect that they had always given. Not once did either belittle me nor throw my situation in my face. One thing for sure, they knew I took good care of their children.

Using my Surge365 membership, I accumulated reward credits and began to use them for our nightly stays. One night comes to mind as I needed to book a night and couldn't because I was quickly spending more than I was earning. I called on a few people to book a night for me; however, we ended up in the Walmart parking lot sleeping in our car. It was pouring down rain. The next day was Monday, and a check was on the way. I told my children to lay back, take their shoes off, and go to sleep. Journey asked me if I was going to sleep too, and as my heart was ripping to shreds, I told her a lie. I said I wasn't sleepy, but I was. This wasn't a 24hr Walmart, so I was praying that no one paid us any mind. About 2 am, I called a friend that lived around the corner and asked if I could stay the night. She welcomed us in with no hesitation. Whew! We were safe again! Monday and a check came. I looked in my back office for more hotels. At this point, I was exhausted. But, I knew that with Surge365, I had tons of opportunity.

As I was taking my children to school, God reminded of his promises. Therefore, instead of me looking and counting the days of how long it would take me to get a place of my own, I started saying I'm just one day closer. When I tell you that was the best self-motivation. I put some pep in my step. I continued to walk around, looking and talking like the person I was becoming and not the person I was familiar with. I was hosting more travel parties and conference calls. The business had not given up on me, so why not go harder! With faith, you don't know when things will happen; you just know they will. There comes a point in life when you have to suck it up and keep going. I had already gone through my worst. What was there to be afraid of? Why was I even worried? I am Tashauna Richardson, and the world was about to hear about it. I had to come to grips that this was all a part of it. Whatever was happening, I had to go through it. My children depended on me. Who's depending on you?

CHAPTER 7: FROM EXTENDED STAY TO EVERWOOD

After residing in the Wyndham by Wingate for about a month or so, I'd finally found a hotel that would give my children some normalcy. I had missed cooking. We were all racking up pounds from eating fast food three times a day. I missed the smell of my fried chicken, rice, and gravy along with macaroni and cheese! Cooking for my children took my mind off a lot of things. Everything I cooked, they loved. I needed a place where I could prepare meals. I looked in my membership and found Extended Stay of America. Equipped with a full kitchen and living room, this was the perfect transitional place.

September 2016, we checked in with all of our belongings. I could afford it, and, as a matter of fact, I could pay by the week. It wasn't a 5-star hotel, but I could cook for them. They asked if there was a pool like the last hotel, and there wasn't. They didn't like that, but mama went to Walmart, purchased groceries, and a fry daddy.

Plates, pots, pans & utensils were already there, but I wanted my own. That first night I went overboard. Hamburger with rice and gravy, sweet peas, and I can't forget the fried chicken! The aroma lit up the entire floor! They ate until they were full and sleepy. I couldn't wait for the next day. Again, I was back in the kitchen. I even had my daughter doing chores like cleaning the bathroom and kitchen. If we were going to be there, then it needed to be clean regardless if housekeeping came in or not. Meanwhile, my business was thriving, and I received an email that I'd been invited to Naples, Florida, to a Regional Builder's Experience with The CEOs of Surge 365.

I was promoted from Regional Builder to National Builder, that meant I was invited, but I needed to pay my own way. Let me tell you; nothing was going to stop me from this opportunity. I felt like the woman with the issue of blood. If I could get there, I knew everything else would fall into place.

It was right before Thanksgiving, and I had no sitter for three of my children. I didn't stress out about it, though. They had never been to Florida, so road trip it was. I googled the time it would take me to drive to Naples, Florida. Eleven hours popped up, but with children, I knew it would be at least a 14-hour ride. I didn't care; I was on my way. I don't think anyone knew my children were with me. We arrived at 1 am after a quick stop at Walmart for snacks. I talked to them that morning and told them I was going to a meeting, and as soon as I got a break, I was going to order food for them. They had plenty of food and snacks in the room with them, but I just had to make sure they were ok. The weather was beautiful, and they caught a glimpse of the pool. As much as I wanted to let them get in, I knew time wouldn't permit. They stayed in the room, watched movies, and never complained. They sent a shuttle bus to pick us up, and I finally felt like, "this is it!" As I promised my children, once we took a break, I ordered food for them, and lots of it! There was more than enough to last them until I returned.

The training was long and intense, but I needed all that they gave me. I soaked up every word. The view was overwhelming! The Grandeeza Country club was no ordinary place! This was a big deal! I'd never been to nor had I been invited to a country club before!

Nevertheless, here I was overlooking this supersized, Olympic style pool and the top of the line bar that accommodated the members. Through the trees, I could see homes on the golf course. People lived there! That wasn't the half of it. Coach Tomer flew in a private chef to serve us one of the best meals I'd ever had! In my mind, I was asking, "what's really going on here?" It was so much at one time that I had to escape outside and go live on my Facebook page to share what I was actually experiencing. Today the "live" has been viewed over 30,000 times.

I was so grateful. Before I knew it, Coach was outside checking on me. I guess someone told him I was out on the balcony crying, well I was, but because I was happy. We took a picture that moment with tears rolling down my face I captured that moment never wanting to forget that feeling.

I couldn't help but think about how I was leaving all of this to return to a hotel. I stopped myself and said, "Not today, Satan, you won't steal my joy!"

I went back in and found my seat. I was sitting at the table with Jennifer and Roderick Houston. One by one, we each shared a few things about ourselves. When they got to me, everyone in unison said we know who you are. I was tickled but humbled at the same time. It was Jennifer's turn, and she mentioned she was a realtor. My heart dropped, and I felt as someone shoved me from the back. It was God saying speak up, and speak up now! In two seconds, I blurted out my situation to her. She never asked one question! She didn't ask why? Some even thought I was mishandling my money. She didn't care. She saw a woman, a mother that needed help, and she could do it. She asked if I wanted to move to Georgia. I responded with I don't care where I live; I can Surge anywhere! She said to give her a few days. I proceeded to eat my dessert, and peace comforted my heart.

As if that day wasn't great the next day, we all were invited to the Founder's home. What!?!? I wasn't ready, but I was ready! Adrienne and I were there for it all! We pulled up to and were greeted with a hug from each founder, and Mrs. Chriss was in the kitchen cooking. For who? For us! Not one time but she fed us twice. Mind blown! The training was about to begin, but Coach said to go on and take a tour of the home. Guess who wanted to get on the elevator? I was too anxious to wait, so I walked up the stairs, and the entire atmosphere of the home was warm and inviting.

After a few selfies and photo ops with other Regional and National Builders, I took my time going downstairs. Each step I told myself you could have this and more. By the time I reached the bottom of the stairs, my level of confidence was at an all-time high.

I looked around and mumbled to myself I do belong here! More than eight hours of training and out of nowhere, the founder of Surge 365 Coach Tomer called me up. He stood up from his Coach's chair, looked me dead in my face with his baby blue eyes, and said, "I want you to be the next Marketing Director." I want you to be the first out of this bunch to do it. He said I know you can do it. Give me a date. I replied, in six months, Coach in six months. I returned to NC on that Sunday night close to midnight. I was tired out my mind, but ready and eager to share with the team what I had learned. Fired up and prepared to get to Marketing Director.

Monday morning, I received a phone call from Jennifer Houston. She said I have a place for you and your children. I started crying. I stopped and said, wait, I don't want to waste your time. My credit is horrible, and I've already spent over $500 in application fees. She responded, did I ask you about your credit? I said, no, you didn't. Her last sentence was I know who you are in this company and you've paved the way for so many, and now it's time for God to bless you and your children. So many could've helped you Tashauna and didn't, she said. I'm glad God landed your need on my table.

Jennifer said I have a 2-bedroom duplex in Villa Rica, Georgia. Usually, when someone says Georgia, we immediately think of Atlanta, but I was headed to a place I'd never heard of. For a pre-celebration, I took my children to Myrtle

Beach for Thanksgiving. My godmother Jean, Mr. Vernon, and Alexis met us there! It was the best Thanksgiving ever. We rolled right on up to Walmart and purchased our Thanksgiving dinner and headed back to the hotel to cook my famous fried chicken and anything else everyone wanted! I was able to take my children on their first helicopter ride, and deep down, it made me feel good to know these were the stories that they would be sharing forever. Here we were doing family stuff. The same things I wanted to do as a child, I was now financially able to offer those experiences to my children.

On December 17th, the children were getting out of school for the holidays. Before I left, I made a decision that ripped my heart out, but I'm glad I made it for the sake of my daughter. I was allowing my child to live with her dad. He was a great father, and his wife was good to her, so why was it so difficult? I had already lost one child, and this felt like I was losing another. Villa Rica wasn't around the corner. I battled with it until it was time to go. I left with Jewel, Sean, and Journey, and we were on the way. We had no idea what life was about to look like, but it had to be better than what's been.

Anxious and excited, I planned on driving straight there with as few stops as possible.

It seemed like it took us forever with the "I gotta pee" to "I'm hungry" Jennifer is waiting on us y'all I kept telling them. Finally, we arrived! I couldn't wait to do life as I knew I could! A 2-bedroom duplex with one bathroom, a tiny kitchen, and the thickest, most comfortable carpet ever. The lights were on. It was warm, and I only had one question for Jennifer, and that was where's Walmart. It's right around the corner. I grabbed a few blankets, pillows, snacks, and we slept so well!

We had no furniture, absolutely nothing! Everything we had before was gone, and I was ok with that! I had a chance to start over. God whispered in my ear, all things NEW! The very next day, I logged onto to Facebook and clicked on the marketplace in search of furniture. Within seconds I found a woman that was having a moving sale in Roswell, Georgia. I went with 700 in my back pocket. When I arrived, I told her I needed everything. I called Jennifer for help, and she sent help. I was able to furnish all but one room. As I was about to leave, she asked if I had just moved to Georgia. Why did you need all this stuff? I told her just a snippet of why, and the way she started looking around to give me more stuff had a river of tears running down my face. She said God is good, and I hugged her to say thank you. She looked at me and said I needed money to fly my daughter and I out to California due to her recent divorce. Her old became my new. As I walked, she handed me more blankets, a toaster, and even asked, if I needed a lamp? Here, take it! I jumped back in my car to head back home, and I cried the entire ride. A few more trips to Walmart and my home was coming together. My children, however, were trying their best to adjust to yet another school. I promised that I wasn't going to do it again. I promise them stability, and I meant it. No, I had enough money to put them in extracurricular activities, and more importantly, we had a place to call home.

Sean wasn't adjusting as well as thought he would. Coming from a year-round to traditional school was a bit much for him. We tried after school tutoring. After he completed the fourth grade, I had to face another difficult decision. I called his dad, and without hesitation, he and his wife welcomed my son into their home. My heart was heavy, but this wasn't about me. My son deserved the best, and this decision was it! Today my son is making 100s so fast I can't keep up with his awards. He's excelling in every area.

It was Jewel, Journey and myself, and I was determined to make sure they stayed on track.

Summers and Christmas breaks were spent with me. In 2017 I had this whole idea of taking them on a Disney cruise for Christmas, but before that, I had to go to

Cancun, Mexico for a convention. Upon my arrival, they all unanimously said they'd rather have a Christmas tree with gifts instead. I remember it as if it was yesterday all the Christmases I was unable to give them, but this year, this time was a different story. My heart leaped with joy, and I rushed to Walmart to find a tree, and I had them to write out a list. I took Javan with me the next day to go shopping, and then Emani the next. And then it hit me like a ton of bricks, that even with children it's the small things that really matter! I cooked all their favorites, and we sat around the tree on the floor with our paper plates, and we had Christmas!

I was getting used to Villa Rica, and my trips back to NC to visit my children were steady. My son Javan is doing exceptionally well in school, and I kind of want to date. I jumped into a long-distance relationship. I thought it was the best for me because I was easily distracted, and I needed to continue building my business. It didn't work out. The signs were there, and I ignored them because I loved him. I dove harder into my business and kept my head down. Today, I'm single and learning to fall in love with myself daily.

After a year of paying my bills on time, I received a call from my realtor Jennifer, and she told me it was time to find a home for my children and me. Honestly, I was ok with where I was. I desired more, but I become comfortable. For five months, we walked through countless homes until one day; we stumbled upon a house that was just listed. We drove up to a two-story brick home, and we walked in. Immediately Jennifer started placing me in this home. The conversation was more personal. She stopped and went live on Facebook to show everyone the possibility.

As we went through every room, she called out our names. She pointed at Journey's room, and the master bedroom was like an apartment within itself. She asked me did I want it? "Absolutely!" I replied. Was it that simple? I don't know. All I know is Jennifer went to work on my behalf. My credit still wasn't in good standing, but she worked miracles. Days went by, and I was itching to call her. I didn't. The call came, and she told me they said no, but she reassured me that God said yes. I stood in his word. They said no again, and this time, she told them to line up with her faith. She was my voice. The next call was to pack up my things; you're moving to Everwood. I screamed, I yelled, and I cried. I fell to my knees and repeated. Right before I left Villa Rica, I hit another $10,000 bonus. God may not come when you want him, but he is always on time.

Today, we reside in a home with five bedrooms, three full baths, and a two-car garage. Don't tell me what God can't do tell me what else He will do! As I began to pull pictures off the wall and pack up our things, once again, God whispered in my ear all things new! I went to the marketplace on Facebook and made a few ads to give things away. Less than two years ago, we checked out of Extended Stay of America, and we were loading up to move to Everwood.

At eight years old, Journey was getting her very own room for the first time. We went to the furniture store, and I told her to run around and get whatever bed she wanted. She chose the bed with lights! I couldn't wait to go to Walmart and start decorating.

Our home has been used for meetups. My grandma stayed a week; my ma has even come a few times. Give me your excuses, and I will show you results. Everwood isn't our final destination. We're just passing through.

For Christmas, my children were all here. We were all under one roof. Oh, the joy of the stomping as they turned cartwheels in the house and the vibrations from the chandelier as Javan was shouting and I can't forget their faces as I prepared a spread of all their favorite foods. Cranton Justice told me that I couldn't be put out of my own home. He also said, "always have a roof for your children." Promise kept.

CHAPTER 8: EMBRACING THE PIT

Nothing hurts more than having your hands lifted, reaching for help, and no one reaches back. You immediately start thinking about everyone you helped along the way only to find out they are nowhere around when you are in need. All I wanted was a little push to get me going. Just like the Dad helping his daughter ride her bike for the first time without training wheels, I needed a little assurance that someone was there to catch me if I should fall. I wanted my mom to see me on prom day and celebrate how beautiful I was. I needed some guidance versus a whooping or harsh punishment as I was making bad decisions. Yes, I knew better than to do some of the things I did, but I sought attention.

I had so much to offer the men who went in and out of my life, but sex was all they wanted from me. I accommodated their wants and needs believing that by doing so,

I would get a little of what I wanted. Bills came as quick as I could blink my eyes. I lived on the "I can put something on it method." My life looked like a Nascar race speeding and going nowhere fast; a roller coaster ride that I couldn't get off!

I was forced to deal with the life I had created for myself. I came to realize that it is ever your situation that's the problem, but it's how you handle your situation that solves the problem. I came to realize that God is not punishing us by keeping us where we are right now. He is preparing us for our next level. Every mishap is a miracle waiting to happen. If we continue to rush God through our trials, I believe it limits our celebration. We are notorious for saying God if you get me through this thing I promise...

Learn to park it, get out the driver's seat, and scoot over to the passenger side. Sometimes we have to learn to be good riders. The view is different when you're not the one driving. The pressure is off. Your only job as a passenger is to enjoy the ride. Will you allow God to be your GPS? If he said to go right, would you do it or would you say I know a quicker route? Life isn't supposed to be a smooth ride; it's full of potholes, inexperienced drivers and folks swerving in your lanes, but your primary focus should be your destination. For every thunderstorm, you have to know that sunshine and rainbows aren't too far away, and sometimes it's a double rainbow.

To be successful, it was necessary to get rid of my old ways, my old friends, and to say goodbye to my old way of thinking. I wanted out so many times, and I pleaded with God to hurry up. Hurry up and fix this. The lights were turned off several times, but God reminded me even in the darkness, he was the light.

I was down for twelve long years. The system told me how to feed my children, where we could live and what we could have. Do you know how it feels to walk in an Eye Care Center, and your child goes to pick up a pair of glasses only to be directed to the Medicaid glasses? Ma'am, these are your son's choices over here.

I realized that wasn't the life I wanted to live, but I continued to live it. There's a difference between a person that accepts life as is versus a person that believes what they're going through is temporary.

I knew God kept me here for a reason, just was too afraid at one point in time to ask Him about my purpose. Did you know that you can be mentally incarcerated; mentally on death row? I'd sentenced myself to life without the possibility of parole. I had embraced every lousy thing that happened to me and claimed it as my own. I now understand that it wasn't about me. God spoke, "it ain't even about you. Your life isn't yours, to begin with. It belongs to Me. I'm your oxygen." When asked, "why then does it feel like I'm suffocating?" He responded, "I'm the one; the only one that can carry you." I asked, "Why does it feel like I'm living on the edge? God, why am I here? I asked to check out. What is it? What do you want with me? God? God, I wanted my son back. That's what I want! What did I do wrong? I wanted someone to love me, and I didn't even love myself. Isn't that ok? Isn't it okay to put others before yourself?" God said, "where did you place me?"

After twelve long, painful years of tragedy after tragedy, I woke up with clarity. I realized that my healing took place in darkness. In the dark, I found my light. The process begins by getting up, standing, and surrendering. The world was revolving, and I evolved in my pit. I stopped looking at my situation and started a mental celebration. My daily affirmations began with I'm just one day closer, and God responded with ALL THINGS NEW. No one understands what they don't know. Physically, all people saw was a single, black, baby mama, with all these kids and baby daddies. God said nope, that's not who you are. You're more than what they think they know. You're my precious cargo, and if they only knew, they would handle you with care. God overturned the judgment I had put on myself. I was free to live.

I found comfort in knowing that healing was taking place as the world was turning with hatred and envy and jealousy. Some of the people that laughed and put in their two cents when I was down are on my team, in my downline. God said for every tear you've cried; the enemy has to pay you back. Two and a half years and over a quarter of a million dollars later, God said payback isn't over.

We rush the seconds, minutes, hours, and we forget all the lessons to be learned as we look for a quick fix. It's not easy changing your life. It's not easy to leave friends behind. It's not easy wondering why you're no longer invited to family functions, but it's mandatory to look forward to get to the next level in life. Skip instead of running sometimes. Slow down and smell the roses (even though I don't like flowers) and then we must pay it forward. Your testimony is the key to unlock deliverance for others.

We must tell the truth when it hurts. We can no longer act like we're ok. You're in control of your day, and not the other way around. Don't be so anxious to heal prematurely. Stay right there. You're never alone. Allow God to love and mold you during the process. Nobody can bring you out of the smoke with no residue better than God. The table is prepared in the pit. Get dressed in your very best. The reservation has been made. The wait is over. Table for one and all of your enemies this way, please. God's very best awaits you in the pit, and he's not serving them until he serves you first. Everything attached to you will win because you didn't abort the process or promise. To appreciate your palace, you must embrace the pit.

CHAPTER 9: THE LAST LINE

There I was, standing at the top of a mountain in Costa Rica. The sun was shining, and the breeze was just right. This wasn't a family vacation. There wasn't a family member in sight to cheer me on. No one snagged my shirt and told me that this was dangerous. No one said Tashauna you need to do your research before zip lining. No one discouraged me from doing this! Standing there at that moment, I realized people that surrounded me were just like me; risk-takers! Wow, what a defining moment!

As I stood there waiting, sweating, and exhausted I said ok Tashauna eight down and one more to go. The sound of the clicks was echoed and magnified. The attendant never asked if I was ready. There's no other choice. Once you start, there's no point of return. The direction is forward. There's no need to look back at what you've conquered so far, and there's no need to give up now. He said, hey you.

Come on; you're next! The home stretch from here. Double-checking to make sure if I'm good to go, he nodded over to the finish line and said; the last line. This was it!

I was tired. This was the ninth line, and it was over after this. Ok, let's go! I gave myself one last pep talk and grabbed the handle one last time. It's at this very moment that most of you have either quit several lines ago or are too afraid to see what's on the other side of finished. What happened? Did you allow those people you call friends and family members to distract you from your destiny? Once an envious person realizes your greatness, they will attack your completion. They've always recognized your greatness, however when you start to take action, so do they. Reality brings them to the conclusion that you're closer to your breakthrough than they are.

Each line was preparing us for the next challenge. We had no blueprint and no idea what was ahead. This group of people I was with didn't care! We had one mission; to finish what we started as a team. There was one long scream after another! Let's not talk about the Tarzan line. I screamed so loud I know it echoed back to the states, but

I did it! Renee did it twice, and her legs were too short for them to grab her the first time. One time was enough for me. Why wasn't she scared? I looked, and she was grinning and laughing in the face of fear! I was with them! We were all scared, but we were all scared together! We all finished together!

The worst race you will even run is a race that you never start. Yeah, you purchased new shoes, and you purchased new running gear, you also made a Facebook post about your new beginning, but who cares when you're out here just looking the part? There's no such thing as fake it 'til you make it! No! Work hard until night becomes day! Roll your sleeves up and get dirty. Pull your hair back and let the sweat drip!

I was too anxious for the unknown to see what was hidden within the trees. I was that little girl again, excited to find out where I was going. The worst-case scenario was that I would fall. If I fell, at least I would have fallen while living! As long as we're living, we're going to endure hardships. Expect the unexpected. Prepare for the worst. There's nothing easy about this thing called LIFE. I've conquered every mountain that's been in my way. I've tackled every obstacle head-on! Did I want to give up? Of course, I did! Did I want to breakdown and die? You're damn right I did! When I realized the fight wasn't my fight alone, I immediately won!

To everything, there is an opposite. With every ending, there is a beginning. Live or die. Have joy or be depressed. I have chosen to have peace. I have come to understand that getting there may cause you to lose many things. It's a daily fight.

Some choose to stay hooked to that man, that failed marriage, that friend that's really an enemy, or to that disturbing thing. I say, free yourself! You didn't come this far just to come this far, and neither did I. You can't stretch with dream killers! Get rid of them TODAY! They will murder your possibilities. What are you willing to carry and what are willing to let go to live your best life? Freedom is expensive when your mind tells you it's not accessible. My Harriet (Renee Toppin) rescued me (because I wanted to be saved) and she could've saved more if they hadn't been so comfortable being bound by lack.

I became my weakest at the last line. Isn't that how it goes? Just when you're at the finish line, the enemy tries his best to keep you from completion. Just at the brink of a breakthrough, all kinds of distractions occur. They want you to fear like them, but you know you're different. They want to tell you that you can't, because they can't and will never put their faith to the test, but you know you can. I made it, and I'll keep on making it.

The team members that were ahead of me were talking about their experience, and I immediately broke down in tears. A circle of completion was formed. Renee covered us in prayer. We all started afraid but willing. We all took a risk. We trusted a line to hold us up. The tears wouldn't stop. Why don't we believe in God the way we believe in everything else? Why is that so difficult? Faith is something we all understand but hardly exercise. How many opportunities have you dismissed because of YOU? Did you know that opportunities never go away, they just go to someone else?

After the tears of joy, I was able to walk down the side of the mountain. Every line represented a struggle. Every line represented a tragedy. Every line represented heartache, but the last line represented FREEDOM. I made it. I survived! I conquered! As long as you're breathing, LIVE. You will regret every chance you don't take. Whatever you can't handle toss it up to GOD!

Do something once a year that scares the hell out of you! I was terrified while on the boat at the tip-top in the Pacific Ocean. The waves were high, and adrenaline pumping! Juliet said, go for it. Come on down. Everyone was cheering me on! This is crazy! Why do people do this? I stood there with my arms stretched out. I never thought about the fact that I couldn't swim. I was surrounded by everyone that has taken risks at some point in their lives. They survived. I was protected. I was FREE! I was FEARLESS!

Zip-lining through the tropical forest, you hear the wind in your ears; it's a roar that never ends. The sound of the rainforest was like a symphony of flutes; the chirping of the birds was so intense it almost felt like they were kissing my ear. You see things moving by you, but they all seem different or a least you see them differently. Each line took me a little further from the beginning. Each line had a different look; a different height, a different scene, and a different scream! The colors! The greens of the trees were not the ones I was used to! They were brighter than anything I had ever seen! From the river flowing beneath our feet to t the sun beaming its sunlight through the beautiful cloudless sky, I was amazed by everything. There was so much to see, but it was moving so fast. There was no going back. There are no do-overs. You have one shot to either stand there and look at everyone else live their dreams or face your fear and go! I chose to find the highest mountain I could find and JUMP!

Celebrate and embrace your now. Hold on tight; you're one day closer to your last line.

DEDICATIONS

These are the lines that saved my life…

    To my #1 Javan Emanuel Richardson; you are my SONshine my only SONshine you make me happy when skies are gray. You'll never know dear how much I love you, please don't take your SONshine away.

To my #2 Jewel Emani Richardson; you are the reason I find peace in all situations. Your laugh makes me laugh. Your beauty exudes from the inside out. Of course, you can buy a little house and move in the backyard with your dog named Mustard.

To my #3 Jordan Faith Hines; you are my burst of endless possibilities. Everything you used to do as a child wowed me. Now, I say oh, I'm not surprised, that's my Jordan! You are my protector. You are full of love and joy. By the way, just because I named you Jordan doesn't mean you are supposed to wear them. Well, when can I stop buying them?

To my #4 Sean Elin Richardson; you are the most laid back, calmest and carefree child I know. You are the reason why look at life with an "It's not bad it'll be alright lens." When you cry, I know that you're hurt because you hardly ever cry. Can't wait to see which NFL team picks you up!

Welcome home, son.

To my #5; Journey Nevaeh Richardson. You are my little shadow. You love everyone in spite of. Such a beautiful, caring, and kind spirit you are! So fashionable and fun! Life will be good to you because you're good to life! #myjourneypoo

To my #6; Ja'Kari Khalil McBride. Six months wasn't long enough...God had other plans for you; for us. You're the reason I chose to live, and on the other side of this life is eternity. We shall meet again my angel.

THANK YOU

My mother: Colavita Tyson

My father: Dandy Richardson

My sisters: Kecia & Shaquanda Richardson

Almena Mayes: Cre8 Your Reality Publishing
Publisher/Editor

Renee Toppin

Nakia Muhammad

Team Vision

Roderick & Jennifer Houston

Kimberly Taylor: Kimazing Photos

Colette Brown: Master Stylist

Gabrielle Bowens: MUA

Jesonya Whitfield

Ashley Neville: Ashlaine Designs LLC

Andrea Zacher

Booking information:

Tashauna Richardson

Iambeautifulthemovement@gmail.com

Or by phone: 252-885-8799

https://m50k-cosmetics.weeblysite.com/

Published by:

Publishing and More...

Contact information:

Cre8YourRealiT@gmail.com

770-821-9000